MW00398707

ROUGH
DIAMOND

ROUGH DIAMOND

★ The Life of ★
Colonel William Stephen Hamilton,
Alexander Hamilton's
★ Forgotten Son ★

A. K. FIELDING

INDIANA UNIVERSITY PRESS

This book is a publication of

Indiana University Press
Office of Scholarly Publishing
Herman B Wells Library 350
1320 East 10th Street
Bloomington, Indiana 47405 USA

iupress.org

© 2021 by A. K. Fielding
All rights reserved

No part of this book may be reproduced or utilized in any form or by any means, electronic or mechanical, including photocopying and recording, or by any information storage and retrieval system, without permission in writing from the publisher. The paper used in this publication meets the minimum requirements of the American National Standard for Information Sciences—Permanence of Paper for Printed Library Materials, ANSI Z39.48-1992.

Manufactured in the United States of America

First printing 2021

Library of Congress Cataloging-in-Publication Data

Names: Fielding, A. K., author.
Title: Rough diamond : the life of Colonel William Stephen Hamilton, Alexander Hamilton's forgotten son / A. K. Fielding.
Other titles: Life of Colonel William Stephen Hamilton, Alexander Hamilton's forgotten son
Description: Bloomington, Indiana : Indiana University Press, [2021] | Includes bibliographical references and index.
Identifiers: LCCN 2020039194 (print) | LCCN 2020039195 (ebook) | ISBN 9780253053947 (hardback) | ISBN 9780253053954 (ebook)
Subjects: LCSH: Hamilton, William Stephen, 1797-1850. | Hamilton family. | Northwest, Old—History. | Frontier and pioneer life—Northwest, Old. | Lawyers—Northwest, Old—Biography.
Classification: LCC F484.3 .F54 2021 (print) | LCC F484.3 (ebook) | DDC 973.4092 [B]—dc23
LC record available at https://lccn.loc.gov/2020039194
LC ebook record available at https://lccn.loc.gov/2020039195

For my Three Stooges: Michael, Tony, and Gabriel

The people of this country have too much wisdom to trample down representative government; and they have delegated this among other acts to be performed by their representatives and we must not shrink therefrom.

William Stephen Hamilton, 1836

Contents

Preface

IN AMERICA, THE EARLY NINETEENTH CENTURY WAS A
time of great upheaval. The election of Thomas Jefferson in 1800 gave
the Jeffersonian Republicans a stronghold over the Federalists led
by Alexander Hamilton, revealing a deep cleavage in the politics of
the American people. The death of Hamilton in 1804, at the hands
of Aaron Burr, sent the Federalists into a downward spiral from
which they never recovered. The gaps between factions continued
to widen as the century progressed, with the rise of the Democratic
Party under Andrew Jackson and the Whig Party under the leadership of Henry Clay. From the age of Jackson to the end of the Mexican
War, America continued to experience changes in its society, culture,
economy, religion, and politics.

The effects of these changes were evident on the frontier as well.
Following the War of 1812, the regions that later became the states
of Illinois and Wisconsin experienced a shift in population as settlers arrived from New England, Missouri, Kentucky, and Tennessee.
Before the war, fur trading supported the region's economy, but that
changed with the growth of lead mining. New lead-mining operations, or "diggings," appeared virtually overnight, making many of
the settlers prosperous, even as many of the Native American tribes
were dislodged from their ancestral lands. William Stephen Hamilton lived through this precarious period in the nation's history.

The toughest part of being the child of a famous person is the pressure to fill the big shoes of the parent. A son of such a parent may be

both famous and obscure. He may be recognizable because of his lineage but may be ignored otherwise. Such is the case with children of the Founding Fathers of America. Only one such man, John Quincy Adams, seems to have left an everlasting impression on the public mind. In contrast, others, such as William, have become lost to history.

William Stephen Hamilton was the sixth child of Alexander Hamilton and Elizabeth Schuyler Hamilton. If we compare William's life to that of his illustrious father, he failed to achieve the same level of political success; yet if we consider that William lived in a period when new ideas were emerging in all areas of society, he becomes an exemplary representative of his time. William's true worth, then, is measurable not as a celebrated politician but as an average man who, along with thousands of others, helped redefine what it meant to be an American.

It is difficult to place William in a particular social order. He was born to a famous New York family, but he chose to live in the wild frontier. His life took various turns and required him to change his future in unconventional ways. The loss of his father when William was seven shaped his youth, and the later estrangement from his family chiseled out a man who was intelligent, hardworking, industrious, and determined. It took physical courage, hardheaded realism, and dedication to settle a town on the frontier, employ misfits, deal with both friendly and hostile Native Americans, engage in politics, and prospect first for lead, then for gold. William accomplished all of these tasks and more, often without any support from anyone, and with gusto.

In studying the early Republic, historians have tried to illuminate the cultural, political, economic, and social issues prevalent during the period with some success. Joyce Appleby's comprehensive study *Inheriting the Revolution: The First Generation of Americans* is based on material collected from two hundred autobiographies, and it credits the rise of American individualism to the second generation of Americans. Daniel Walker Howe's extraordinary work *What Hath God Wrought: The Transformation of America, 1815–1848* weaves together the intricate stories of average Americans and those belonging to the elite society during the early Republic. Gordon Wood's *Empire of Liberty: A History of the Early Republic, 1789–1815* focuses on the experiences of the upper class during this period. Yet most of the studies covering this period either focus on well-known Americans or make sweeping generalizations about the experiences of the pioneers.

This book examines events that took place on the frontier during the time of the early Republic through the lens of an obscure yet exceptional man, William Stephen Hamilton. Although the name Hamilton itself should have drawn respect and admiration, such was not always the case on the frontier. During the early Republic, the Jacksonians ruled the day in almost all of America. William's own brothers were able to attain good positions in the government, working for the popular Jackson administration, but William, like many others, turned to the West to establish himself.

William has remained unknown to people because records about him are scarce. Moreover, historians have overlooked him because he was less famous than many of his contemporaries. Just one historian, Sylvan J. Muldoon, attempted to give a full-length biography of William: *Alexander Hamilton's Pioneer Son: Life and Times of Colonel William Stephen Hamilton*, published in 1930. Muldoon's work left gaps in William's story that required fresh research.

William was tight-lipped about his personal life. He left no known journal or diary. Before he left the Midwest for California, he seems to have left much of his personal belongings, including personal papers, with a neighbor in Wisconsin, but these items either have not survived or are yet to be located. Fortunately, some of his personal and business letters have survived and helped in patching together his life for this book. Contemporary documents including legal records, newspaper articles, journals, and letters are the bulk of primary sources for this study and offer some insight as to William's appearance, business acumen, political stance, and character. Aside from such sources, the only way to truly find out more about William is to study his life through the period in which he lived.

In "Broken Beginnings," William's life unfolds, starting with his parentage and early life in New York. William witnesses the death of his father, and its devastating impact on his family, just short of his seventh birthday. Despite being born to a prestigious family, William is unable and often unwilling to benefit from the many advantages of his family's association with high society.

"The Man" explores the reasons that William chose to move to the Midwest. It delves deeper into his character and personality. "Life in Illinois" focuses on William's life as a lawyer and politician in that state. William is the defense attorney in the case of Nom-A-Que, a Native American man accused of murdering a Frenchman in Peoria. William also tries to run for political office for the first time, in Sangamon County. The close ties between William and his mother, and other individuals in his life, are discussed at length. William helps welcome his father's dear friend Marie-Joseph Paul Yves Roch Gilbert du Motier, Marquis de Lafayette, on his return visit to America in 1824. He participates in the Winnebago War in 1827. The chapter also debunks myths about William's confrontation with his father's killer, Aaron Burr, in Saint Louis, Missouri.

"Black Hawk War" covers William's service as a volunteer in the militia in Iowa County, Michigan Territory. He constructs and oversees the building of Fort Hamilton to provide protection for the miners and settlers around Hamilton's Diggings, a mining camp that he founded on his arrival in southern Wisconsin. He also leads the Winnebagos, Menominees, and Sioux to scout for the US military during the war. The chapter also discusses the possible meeting between William and Abraham Lincoln.

William's relocation to the lead region is the focus of "Gray Gold." He is one of the earliest pioneers to settle in the mining district. Here, William makes lifelong friends, such as lawyer and businessman Cyrus Woodman, and enemies, such as politician James Duane Doty. William's life after the war is also discussed. "Taming the Frontier" focuses on the heated political atmosphere in the Wisconsin Territory. William also settles new towns in Wisconsin. His mother, Elizabeth Hamilton; her daughter, William's younger sister, Eliza Hamilton Holly; and Eliza's husband, Sidney Holly, arrive at Hamilton's Diggings to visit William. "El Dorado" covers William's journey to California during the 1849 Gold Rush, and "Dead End" describes the year he spent in California prospecting for gold. The chapter also analyzes the cause and date of his death.

Why did Alexander Hamilton's son relocate hundreds of miles away from his home, family, and friends? Why did he never return back home to New York to live out the remainder of his days? How did he survive the untamed frontier? What contributions did he make to society? Did he leave it better or worse for the next generation? I desired to answer these questions not just to understand William but also to understand the period that molded a unique American mindset—one that embraced the principles of perseverance, determination, and ingenuity. In studying William's life, the aim was not only to further the knowledge of the Hamilton family of New York and enhance our understanding of the impact of the early Republic on the American pioneers in the Midwest but also to recognize the unique American ethos of the period, which still resonates with us today.

For the sake of maintaining originality, all quotes have been kept in their original format.

Acknowledgments

THE SEED OF THIS BOOK GERMINATED IN 2010 WHEN I began to research Rachel Faucette Lavien and her son Alexander Hamilton. I was trying to find similarities between the mother and son. Through the materials I gathered, I found out about a photograph that was purported to be of two of Alexander Hamilton's sons: Philip and William. Out of curiosity, believing that the same photograph could only be of one of the two men, I delved deeper. As more and more evidence came into my hands, I became convinced that the photograph was the image of William. I later published my findings in the *Illinois Heritage* magazine in 2014. Moreover, I determined to turn my work into a full-length biography.

It has been a long journey to bring William's biography to publication. None of it would be possible without the enormous support I have received through that journey to tell his story. The first person I want to thank is professor and dear friend Dr. Valerie McKito for her guidance and encouragement at the University of Nebraska–Kearney. She read and reread my work many times and gave me the courage to keep going. Simone Munson at the Wisconsin Historical Society gave me the crucial assistance I needed when I was conducting research both off-site and when I visited WHS. Author Ron Chernow graciously responded to my messages when I was researching William's photograph and sent me to Linda R. Baumgarten, curator at Colonial Williamsburg Foundation, who verified my hunch about

William's clothing and thereby confirmed my belief that the person in the photograph was not Phillip but William. Thank you to Bill Furry at the Illinois State Historical Society, who gave me my first break in publishing the story about William's photograph.

Dr. James Cornelius at the Abraham Lincoln Presidential Library and Museum went above and beyond, oftentimes digging for primary sources, to supply me with the information that I needed. At one point in my research, I came across a major glitch in a source that was smoothed out with fantastic sleuthing from Deb Bier at the Peoria Public Library. Elena Smith at the California State Library provided much-needed help in tracking down sources about William's life in California. Clayton Higbee at the Tippecanoe County Public Library worked diligently to provide me with the hard-to-find sources I needed during research. Lisa Kelly at the Nebraska Library Commission was elemental in providing me with an extremely important primary source needed to complete this book. Douglas Hamilton, a Hamilton descendant, was generous with his time and provided crucial information about the Hamilton family. Rand Scholet, founder of the Alexander Hamilton Awareness Society, read my manuscript and gave generous support and feedback. Thank you to my editor, Ashley Runyon, who believed in this book, and her assistant Anna Francis, who worked diligently to provide me with all the help I needed. I am deeply grateful to dear friend and author Richard Brookhiser, who read my manuscript, gave me generous feedback, offered me encouragement, and always gave me full support to keep pressing forward. Above all, I want to thank my family for their unflinching faith in me; without them, this book would never have begun.

ROUGH
DIAMOND

ONE

Broken Beginnings

"[I] HAD RATHER HAVE BEEN HUNG IN THE 'LEAD MINES' than to have lived in this miserable hole."[1] Lying on a small mattress on the floor of the dark, filthy room he rented in a two-story building on J Street in Sacramento, California, Colonel William Stephen Hamilton struggled once more to ward off chills and acute pain. Paralysis was beginning to settle into his exhausted body.[2] On the muddy street below, people continued to discuss California's recent statehood and the governor's proclamation calling for a new state capital.[3] In their everyday hustle and bustle of hunting for gold, few realized that an ill man lying above was the son of one of the nation's Founding Fathers, Alexander Hamilton.

Born on August 4, 1797, William had an adventurous spirit from a young age. His father called him his "little Arab" with affection, possibly because he acquired a deep tan from playing outdoors often. Once, he held a snake in his hands and chased a friend around the lawn of his family home, the Grange, in New York.[4] The backwoods near the Hudson River behind the Grange must have made an ideal playground for a young boy who was in his element when surrounded by nature. His mother, Elizabeth Hamilton, who enjoyed nature herself, probably influenced his deep love for the outdoors. During the Revolutionary War, Elizabeth had made quite an impression on Tench Tilghman, a young aide-de-camp serving under General George Washington. On August 23, 1775, at an excursion with friends to the Cohoes Falls in New York, Tilghman watched Elizabeth with admiration and noted in his journal, "I fancy Miss Schuyler has been used to ramble over and climb grounds of this sort for she disdained all assistance and made herself merry at the distress of the other Ladies."[5]

William's neighbor in the Midwest, Theodore Rodolf, described him as a man of "medium height, stout, well built, and of robust health, able to bear the hardships of frontier life" who "socially . . . was pleasant, but not communicative, and left the impression of a rather cold and distant man."[6] His great nephew, Edgar Hamilton, noted that he "was a man of medium stature and spare form, his features were small, hair brown and complexion light." He had a "high" voice and spoke "rapidly."[7] Later in life, Edgar Hamilton wrote in his autobiography that William "was a man of small stature, blue eyes, auburn hair, and intellectual face."[8] When William was older, another contemporary, Dr. Israel Shipman Pelton Lord, recorded in his journal that William was "small, active, smart looking man, apparently fifty, and was once undoubtedly a very handsome man."[9] Of all the Hamilton children, William possessed his father's handsome features and magnetic personality.[10]

As with most of the men in his family, William loved "manly exercise"; he was also "fond of horseback riding" and kept "physical strength and suppleness until quite old age."[11] Once when William was escorting his friends across Wisconsin on horseback, one of the riders found him to be an "agreeable companion . . . but a most desperate rider" and said that even though they were all "well mounted . . . he sometimes nearly distanced us."[12] His youngest brother, Philip Hamilton, thought William possessed amicability, courage, and "manliness."[13] In the one surviving portrait of him, William looks on the observer with confidence.[14] There is a sense of mischief in his smile but in his eyes there is also a kindness that he generously bestowed on people during his lifetime.

For the longest time, a mystery has surrounded this particular portrait: a black-and-white photograph of a portrait painted sometime in the nineteenth century. The Wisconsin Historical Society maintains that the portrait is of William. However, for over a hundred years, much of the historical community has presented the same photograph as the image of William's eldest brother, Philip Hamilton. So who truly is the subject of the photograph: William or Philip? Determining the identity of the subject in the photograph became imperative and provided an incredible opportunity to put the long-standing question to rest.

My research began with a systematic search of all historical institutions that use the Wisconsin Historical Society's photograph. Noting whom they listed as the subject and credited as their source could create a trail leading to the oldest source for the photograph. This method soon grew cumbersome and frustrating, as most of them listed the same source for the photograph, *The Intimate Life of Alexander Hamilton*, published in 1910, written by none other than Alexander Hamilton's grandson Allan McLane Hamilton. The book stated the photograph was of a portrait of Philip Hamilton. While this seemed conclusive, the Wisconsin Historical Society disagreed, and as they appeared to have the original copy of the photograph and the most relevant documents in relation to William, it made sense to check for any information they had about the origins. Information was exchanged and extensive research conducted, but the Wisconsin Historical Society did not have any information on the original painting. Contacting William's home, the Hamilton Grange in New York, brought forth the same response: the photo was of a portrait painting of Philip, and the location of the original painting was unknown.

The next step involved turning to information on Alexander Hamilton in the hope that his biographers may have referred to his sons and the photograph. Fortunately, major historians have done extensive work on the life of Hamilton and referenced both the sons and the photograph, but the results were dismal. Ron Chernow's *Alexander Hamilton* (2004) identified the subject in the photograph as Philip Hamilton. Additionally, Willard Sterne Randall's book *Alexander Hamilton: A Life* (2003) also showed the same photograph and listed the young man as Philip Hamilton. Both historians attributed the image to the 1910 biography of Hamilton by Allan McLane

Hamilton, and if anyone knew the subject of the photograph, who better than the grandson of Alexander Hamilton? The only exception to this ruling appeared in a book published in 1903 titled *The Black Hawk War*, by Frank E. Stevens, who identified the same photograph as William S. Hamilton. *The Black Hawk War*, published seven years before *The Intimate Life of Alexander Hamilton*, seemed to have information that aligned with that of the Wisconsin Historical Society.

Another method of identifying the subject was the photograph itself. Philip was born on January 22, 1782, and William was born on August 4, 1797. With an age difference of fifteen years between the two brothers, if a reliable date for the portrait could be found, it would be possible to determine which brother was the subject of the painting. The photograph depicted a young man; therefore, whether the portrait belonged to Philip or William, it originated when the person was in his late teens or early twenties. I closely inspected the details of the photograph to see if any clues would help determine the identity of the subject.

The young man's features, including his hairstyle and clothing in particular, were the starting point. With a gap of more than a decade between the two brothers, I thought the style of the young man's clothing could reveal something of significance. A search for men's clothing from the nineteenth century revealed gentlemen's fashion trends in the Regency and Victorian eras. I compared this to the style from eighteenth century, the Georgian period. The idea was quite simple: If the photograph belonged to Philip, then his hairstyle and clothing would reflect the Georgian period of the late eighteenth century. Anything beyond 1801 would be too late in this case. On the other hand, if the clothing and hairstyle reflected the early to mid-nineteenth century, it could only be William because Philip was already dead by then. Further research with the help of the Colonial Williamsburg Foundation revealed that the clothing worn by the young man in the photograph indeed reflected nineteenth-century fashion.

Another positive moment occurred when the Wisconsin Historical Society verified that the photograph was a copy sent to the society along with a letter from Philip Hamilton (younger brother of

William) from Poughkeepsie, New York, dated February 1880. The letter identified William as the subject of the photograph and stated: "The last subject relates to any likenesses of my brother [William] and I am gratified to have it in my power, to supply the society, as I promised to you yesterday, an enlarged Indian ink photograph from an Ivory miniature which has been in my possession since my sister's death."[15] The photograph itself had clear marking identifying the subject as William, and the handwriting matched the accompanying letter signed by Philip. The confirmation and proof from the Wisconsin Historical Society was enough to positively identify the young man in the portrait as William and not his eldest brother, Philip, resolving the mystery once and for all.

William's father, Alexander Hamilton, spent his youth on the island of Nevis in the British West Indies, under challenging circumstances. His mother, Rachel Faucett Lavien, had left her husband and firstborn child under questionable conditions. When she met James Hamilton, Hamilton's father, they were unable to get married because of the unresolved issues related to her previous marriage.[16] Hamilton and his older brother, James Jr., were both born and raised as illegitimate children. As if the fates were set against them, James Sr. left the young family to fend for themselves in 1766. Two years later, Rachel died from a terrible fever, making both boys orphans at a time when they most needed the guidance of parents.[17]

After the loss of his mother to a fatal disease that almost killed him as well, Hamilton had minimal support from extended relatives. In order to survive in a place destitute of any relations, Hamilton and his brother worked as apprentices for local businesses. Hamilton tried his hand at clerking for the local mercantile business of Beekman and Cruger. There, he learned many business and economics principles, which he improved on in later years.

As a young man, Hamilton yearned to escape the hopelessness he felt living on the island of Saint Croix, and he pined for more out of life. In a letter written to his best friend, Edward Stevens, he cried out in desperation: "To confess my weakness, Ned, my ambition is prevalent that I contemn the grov'ling and condition of a Clerk of the like, to which my Fortune &c. condemns me and would willingly risk my life tho' not my Character, to exalt my Station." Yet, even as a teenager, Hamilton was a determined young man, who said, "Im confident, Ned, that my Youth excludes me from any hopes of immediate Preferment nor do I desire it, but I mean to prepare the way for futurity."[18]

Hamilton took full advantage of any opportunity he found to educate himself. He was a voracious reader, he spoke French with ease, and his thirst for knowledge remained unquenchable. Already, he had developed a powerful writing style, which earned him his ticket out of Saint Croix. Although James had abandoned his family more than six years earlier, Hamilton still found a way to keep in touch with his father. A letter Hamilton wrote to his father describing the Saint Croix hurricane of August 31, 1772, was published in a local paper, and it caused a sensation in his town. As a result, many of his neighbors gathered together to help fund his education in the colonies.[19] In due time, Hamilton was able to realize his dream, as his strong business acumen, determination, and knack for writing made him more than capable of handling the busyness of his new home: New York City.

Hamilton was a penniless immigrant with a questionable background when he first arrived to attend the Academy at Elizabethtown in October 1772. He stayed there until the summer of 1773. He then went on to become a private student at King's College in the fall of 1773. Hamilton's "illegitimate" birth in 1757 remained a sore subject throughout his life. Some of his contemporaries were relentless in administering their low opinion of him in both public and private. In 1797, John Adams, soon to be second president of the United States, wrote to his wife, Abigail, "Hamilton I know to be proud Spirited, conceited, aspiring Mortal always pretending to Morality, with as debauched Morals as old Franklin who is more his Model than any one I know." Adams insisted that Hamilton was unscrupulous and "as great an Hypocrite as any in the U.S." and that he found "his Intrigues" despicable.[20]

It is notable that despite facing harsh criticism throughout his life, Hamilton managed to break through the barriers and achieve a level of success that was uncommon for someone with his background in the eighteenth century. When he was a young student alone in New York, Hamilton's quick wit, bravery, and determination helped him earn immediate upper-class connections with Elias Boudinot, who later served as president of the Congress of the Confederation, and William Livingston, who later became the first governor of New Jersey.

The breakout of the Revolutionary War interrupted Hamilton's education. He signed up for military service as an artillery captain from New York on March 14, 1776. Hamilton supervised the construction of a small fort on Bayard's Hill to defend New York from the incoming British invasion. General George Washington arrived with the Continental army in April to lead the fight against the British for New York.

At the Battle of Brooklyn on August 27, 1776, the British defeated Washington's Continental army in New York. Washington fought back at the Battle of Harlem and earned a victory over the British on September 16, only to be defeated by them again on October 28 at the Battle of White Plains. Fortunately, he escaped with his men and remained under cover in the wilderness. During Washington's struggle with Congress for extra support for his men, Hamilton remained close by to offer his assistance. He soon became an important part of Washington's "family" and served as one of the general's aides-de-camp.[21]

It was in 1779 when serving under the command of Washington that Hamilton began to consider the possibility of settling down. For this, he sought the help of his friend and fellow officer John Laurens. Laurens was the son of South Carolina's elite planter Henry Laurens, and he had joined Washington's family in October 1777. Hamilton wrote to his friend in April 1779: "Now my Dear as we are upon the subject of wife, I empower and command you to get me one in Carolina. Such a wife as I want will, I know, be difficult to be found, but if you succeed, it will be the stronger proof of your zeal and dexterity." Hamilton then listed the specific qualities he sought in his future mate: "Take her description—She must be young, handsome (I lay most stress upon a good shape) sensible (a little learning will do), well bred (but she must have an aversion to the word ton) chaste and tender (I am enthusiast in my notions of fidelity and fondness) of some good nature, a great deal of generosity (she must neither love money nor scolding, for I dislike equally a termagent and an oeconomist)." He was confident that he had the power to persuade the right woman to his way of thinking: "In politics, I am indifferent what side she may be of; I think I have arguments that will easily convert her to mine. As to religion a moderate stock will satisfy me. She must believe in god and hate a saint." Perhaps he was thinking about his own mother's misfortune when he broached the subject of money: "As to fortune, the larger stock of that the better." He was referring to his future wife's needs as much as to his own when discussing money, which he felt was "an essential ingredient to happiness in this world." He was unsure about his ability to amass great wealth; therefore, his prospective wife should "bring at least a sufficiency to administer to her own extravagancies."[22]

His wish was soon granted. In 1780, Elizabeth Schuyler entered Hamilton's life, and he knew that she fit his requirements of an ideal wife just as he had envisioned. Elizabeth Schuyler was born on August 9, 1757. She was the second daughter of General Philip Schuyler and Catherine Van Rensselaer, of a prominent New York family.[23] Elizabeth's father was a Revolutionary War hero, and her mother came from a family of wealth and prestige. Far from being a coquette, Elizabeth was an intelligent, strong, and capable young woman.[24] She was fond of nature and enjoyed going for long walks. Even in her old age, this habit remained; when she visited her son William, she insisted on going for long walks, often unescorted, in the untamed frontier of the Midwest.[25]

During their courtship, Hamilton was unsure about his ability to provide Elizabeth with the many comforts of life she was accustomed to as a Schuyler. He urged her to consider her future as "a poor man's wife" and asked her if she had considered a simple life of "home spun preferable to a brocade and the rumbling of a wagon wheel to the musical rattling of a coach" and if she could cope with having to "see with perfect composure your old acquaintances flaunting it in gay life, tripping it along in elegance and splendor, while you hold an humble station and have no other enjoyments than the sober comforts of a good wife?" Moreover, he asked if she would be willing to "cheerfully plant turnips" with him. Hamilton begged Elizabeth to "examine well your heart. And in doing it, don't figure to yourself a cottage in romance, with the spontaneous bounties of nature courting you to enjoyment." He gave her plenty of leverage to reject him as her suitor: "Don't imagine yourself a shepherdess, your hair embroidered with flowers a crook in your hand tending your flock under a shady tree, by the side of a cool fountain, your faithful shepherd sitting near and entertaining you with gentle tales of love." He also urged her to be practical in her thinking about her future with him: "These are pretty dreams and very apt to enter into the heads of lovers when they think of a connection without the advantage. But they must not be indulged. You must apply your situation to real life, and think how you should feel in scenes of which you may find examples every day."[26]

The letter provides insight into Hamilton's feelings about marriage in general, which must have prompted painful memories of his unstable life as a youth. It also indicates that he needed Elizabeth to assure him that their marriage would last a lifetime. Was he thinking of his mother, who had left her first husband? Did he think that it might happen to him? Or did he remember his father leaving his mother to provide for herself and their children? Whatever his thoughts, Hamilton need not have worried, because Elizabeth proved to be a dedicated wife through the course of their marriage and even after his death. She worked with diligence to ensure that Hamilton's papers were preserved and available to the nation they both loved. Not just Elizabeth but her entire family embraced this immigrant with open arms. Hamilton must have been quite charming and charismatic to woo not just his beloved but also his in-laws.

On December 14, 1780, Alexander Hamilton and Elizabeth Schuyler were married at the Schuyler mansion in Albany, New York. The majority of people who attended the ceremony were Schuyler friends and relatives. In sharp contrast, the groom stood alone.[27] Yet it was a happy occasion for both bride and groom. Considering his background, Hamilton must have been excited about starting his life with his new bride.

During the course of their marriage, Alexander and Elizabeth Hamilton had eight children. Their eldest son, Philip Hamilton, was born on January 22, 1782. A succession of other children followed: Angelica, September 25, 1784; Alexander, May 16, 1786; James Alexander, April 14, 1788; John Church, August 22, 1792; William Stephen, August 4, 1797; Eliza, November 20, 1799; Philip (younger), June 2, 1802.[28]

As the firstborn, Philip was the apple of their eyes, and both parents were optimistic that their son would have a bright future. In a letter to Richard Kidder Meade, Hamilton rushed to write about his happy news on Philip's birth. His excitement as a new father is obvious: "He is truly a very fine young gentleman, the most agreeable in his conversation and manners of any I ever knew—nor less remarkable for his intelligence and sweetness of temper. You are not to imagine by my beginning with his mental qualifications that he is defective in personal." Hamilton was already proud of his son's good looks and demeanor: "It is agreed on all hands, that he is handsome, his features are good, his eye is not only sprightly and expressive but it is full of benignity. His attitude in sitting is by connoisseurs esteemed graceful and he has a method of waving his hand that announces the future orator."[29]

Years later, Hamilton wrote with affection to Philip, who was then attending school: "I received with great pleasure My Dear Philip the letter which you wrote me last week. Your Master also informs me that you recited a lesson the first day you began, very much to his satisfaction. I expect every letter from him will give me a fresh proof of your progress." Again, the warmth, pride, and hope that Hamilton placed in Philip are hard to miss: "For I know you can do a great deal, if you please, and I am sure you have too much spirit not to exert yourself, that you may make us every day more and more proud of you." Even Philip's mother joined her husband in encouraging her son: "Your Mama and myself were very happy to learn that you are pleased with your situation and content to stay as long as shall be thought for your good." Then Hamilton offered sound advice to his firstborn son before closing the letter: "A promise must never be broken; and I never will make you one, which I will not fulfil as far as I am able.... A good night to my darling son."[30]

When Philip was fifteen, he suffered from a severe case of typhus fever, which tried the energy and fortitude of both parents. Unsure about the outcome of his beloved child's illness, Hamilton worked with the physician to revive his son and to calm his frantic wife at the same time.[31] Yet nothing could have prepared the two parents for the impending doom.

At the age of nineteen, Philip and his friend Stephen Price became involved in a heated argument with a young Republican named George I. Eacker. On July 4, 1801, Eacker had made a grand speech about Hamilton's possible use of the army to oppress Republicans. Insults were thrown on both sides, followed by a challenge to an arranged duel between the parties. Eacker and Price survived their duel. When it was Philip's turn the next morning, Eacker's bullet found its mark. Philip died in agony the next day.[32] On March 29, 1802, Hamilton wrote to Benjamin Rush that the loss was the "most afflicting of my life."[33] Hamilton may have never recovered from losing his firstborn son, and he agonized over the loss until his own death three years later.

To be sure, Hamilton loved Philip a great deal, but he also shared a deep regard for all his children. In a letter to his daughter Angelica, Hamilton offered advice on proper behavior, as he had done with Philip: "We hope you will in every respect behave in such a manner as will secure to you the good-will and regard of all those with whom you are. If you happen to displease any of them, be always ready to make a frank apology. But the best way is to act with so much politeness, good manners, and circumspection, as never to have occasion to make any apology. Your mother joins in best love to you. Adieu, my very dear daughter."[34]

After years of separation from his relatives, Hamilton wrote a letter of introduction to his uncle, William Hamilton, mentioning his family with a father's pride: "It is impossible to be happier than I am in a wife and I have five Children, four sons and a daughter, the eldest son somewhat passed fifteen, who all promise well, as far as their years permit and yield me such satisfaction."[35] Years later, Hamilton's son James A. Hamilton reminisced about his father's "gentle" and "affectionate" nature toward all of his children.[36] Considering his own rocky start in the world, it is evident that Hamilton loved his children and that he was a loving and involved parent.

The eldest daughter of Alexander and Elizabeth Hamilton, and their second child, Angelica, was a beauty who loved music. After the sudden death of her elder brother, Philip, Angelica lost all control of her faculties, and she spent the remainder of her life talking about her brother as if he were still alive.[37] In an effort to bring her out of her mental illness, in 1802 Hamilton wrote a letter to his friend and fellow Federalist Party member Charles Cotesworth Pinckney, making known Angelica's childlike "request, which is for three or four of your peroquets. She is very fond of birds."[38] But nothing helped her come back to reality. Angelica lived with her mental illness until her death at the age of seventy-three.

The second son, Alexander, studied at Columbia University and graduated in 1804. After graduation, he became a lawyer and then traveled to Europe to fight for the Duke of Wellington's army against Napoleon's forces in Portugal. Later, he fought as Captain of the Forty-First Regiment of Infantry for the US Army against Britain in the War of 1812. He became the US district attorney for New York, and in 1834 he represented the second wife of Aaron Burr, Eliza Bowen Jumel, when she divorced Burr for infidelity.

James Alexander also attended Columbia University, and he graduated in 1805. He too fought in the War of 1812. After the war, he served as secretary of state and as a diplomat for the United States under presidents Andrew Jackson and Martin Van Buren. He later became a US attorney for the southern district of New York.

Like his elder brothers, John Church attended Columbia University, graduating in 1809. He studied law and fought in the War of 1812. His most important contribution to history was the publication of his father's papers.

The youngest daughter of Hamilton and Elizabeth, Eliza, shared many of her mother's qualities. She was a strong, intelligent, and affectionate young woman. She remained a pillar of strength for her mother until Elizabeth's death. She was also close to her brother William, and the two kept a regular correspondence. It is unfortunate that the letters they shared have since disappeared or been destroyed.[39] Eliza married a New York merchant named Sidney A. Holly. After her mother sold the Grange following her father's death, Eliza moved in with her husband, her mother, her brother Alexander, and his wife in a townhouse in the East Village of Manhattan, New York. Eliza lived there until the death of her husband, after which she moved to Washington, DC, with her mother and lived there until her mother's death on November 9, 1854.

Philip (younger), or "Lil Phil," named after his eldest brother, struggled through life and had minimal education in law compared to most of his elder brothers. He managed to procure a position as an assistant to the US attorney. Later, he spent the remainder of his life in New York helping the less fortunate.[40]

Out of all their children, Alexander and Elizabeth Hamilton's sixth child, William Stephen Hamilton, most resembled his father in both physical characteristics and mannerisms.[41] Perhaps the one exception was Philip the elder, who was dead by the time William came of age. William dedicated much of his childhood to astute observations of his father's work ethic, which he tried to emulate as an adult.[42]

Hamilton worked on building a house for his family in New York, and on its completion he named it the Grange after his father's ancestral home in Scotland. The property was located on a beautiful wooded lot near the Hudson River.[43] It was the Hamiltons' first official home, where Hamilton and Elizabeth settled down to raise their brood of children. Away from the stressful political life in the city, the home was a welcome reprieve for Hamilton and his family. Here, he spent many a day playing the piano and singing duets with his daughter Angelica. On other occasions, he spent time cultivating his ever-growing garden, lush with various varieties of fruits, plants, and his thirteen sweet gum trees.[44]

Elizabeth was a good mother to their children. Years later, James A. Hamilton recollected that his mother sat at the breakfast table each morning to make butter sandwiches for the children as they read from the Bible. Then the boys had their breakfast with Hamilton before leaving for school.[45] At least during these times, the Hamilton family had a happy home.

Elizabeth was also a pious and compassionate woman who was always ready to help others. The charity work she did to help the needy and the poor is now receiving some recognition through the efforts of scholars and organizations interested in the Hamilton family. Elizabeth was a charming, graceful, simple, but spirited woman who maintained her energy and faculties until the end of her time.[46] She also remained loyal to Hamilton until her own death. Years after Hamilton's death, James Monroe tried to call on Elizabeth, but she informed him, "Mr. Monroe, if you have come to tell me you repent, that you are sorry, for the misrepresentations and slanders, and the stories you circulated against my dear husband, if you have come to say this, I understand it. But, otherwise, no lapse of time, no nearness to the grave, makes any difference."[47] Time and space were unable to remove her deep regard for her husband, and her relationship with her son William also remained strong until the end.[48]

Hamilton's indiscretion and adulterous relationship with a woman named Maria Reynolds brought unfortunate consequences for the whole family. The affair was exceptionally painful because when it was revealed to the world, Elizabeth was heavily pregnant with William. The scandal began in 1797, when James Callender, a Philadelphia journalist, published a series of pamphlets attacking Hamilton's reputation by suggesting that he was involved in the speculation of public funds with a man named James Reynolds. More concerned with his public image than his personal life, Hamilton took up the challenge and issued his own pamphlet, clearing his name from any involvement in the charges. He was forthright as he explained, "A just pride with reluctance stoops to a formal vindication against so despicable a contrivance and is inclined rather to oppose to it the uniform evidence of an upright character." Then Hamilton noted that his true crime was his engagement in an affair with Reynolds's wife, Maria, in 1791: "The charge against me is a connection with one James Reynolds for purposes of improper pecuniary speculation. My real crime is an amorous connection with his wife, for a considerable time with his privity and connivance, if not originally brought on by a combination between the husband and wife with the design to extort money from me." He was ashamed for having hurt his wife: "This confession is not made without a blush. I cannot be the apologist of any vice because the ardour of passion may have made it mine. I can never cease to condemn myself for the pang, which it may inflict in a bosom eminently intitled to all my gratitude, fidelity and love." He hoped "that bosom will approve, that even at so great an expence, I should effectually wipe away a more serious stain from a name, which it cherishes with no less elevation than tenderness."[49]

The Reynolds affair was just one of Hamilton's problems. The following years saw an increase in political battles between the Federalists and Jeffersonian Republicans that intensified his wavering position in political circles. With the admission of his extramarital affair, he had become more vulnerable. Yet, even at the risk of watching his party dwindle, Hamilton encouraged Thomas Jefferson's ticket for the election of 1800 instead of risking a win for Burr, a man he considered dangerous.

Somehow, Hamilton managed to live for the next three years despite his struggles. In 1804, he met his end in the same striking manner as his son Philip, in a duel, at the hands of none other than his nemesis, Burr. As if he foresaw the outcome of the duel, he prepared a last love letter to his wife days in advance: "This letter, my very dear Eliza, will not be delivered to you, unless I shall first have terminated my earthly career; to begin, as I humbly hope from redeeming grace and divine mercy, a happy immortality." His family remained the last focus of his thoughts, but so was his pride: "If it had been possible for me to have avoided the interview, my love for you and my precious children would have been alone a decisive motive. But it was not possible, without sacrifices which would have rendered me unworthy of your esteem. I need not tell you of the pangs I feel, from the idea of quitting you and exposing you to the anguish which I know you would feel. Nor could I dwell on the topic lest it should unman me."

In a last urgent request, Hamilton begged Elizabeth to depend on her faith in God: "The consolations of Religion, my beloved, can alone support you; and these you have a right to enjoy. Fly to the bosom of your God and be comforted. With my last idea; I shall cherish the sweet hope of meeting you in a better world. Adieu best of wives and best of Women. Embrace all my darling Children for me."[50]

On the morning of July 11, 1804, Hamilton left New York with Nathaniel Pendleton and Dr. David Hosack to fight his last battle with Burr at Weehawken, New Jersey. His brother-in-law, John Baker Church, had lent Hamilton the same pistols that Philip had used in his duel with Eacker in 1801. Burr arrived with his friend, William P. Van Ness. Both Hamilton and Burr had come prepared to fight in what would become the most infamous duel in the nation's history.

The men took the necessary steps according to the rules. Pendleton called out for them to shoot. Two shots were fired, creating a loud bang that echoed throughout the park. The smell of gunpowder filled the air. When the smoke cleared, Hamilton lay on the ground, writhing in pain, never to stand again. Burr's bullet had fatally wounded Hamilton.

The next day, Hamilton lay breathing his last on a bed in the home of William Bayard, the director of the Bank of New York. It was his family's final opportunity to see him alive. The room was crowded with friends and relatives there to offer support and to grieve the dying man. William and his siblings were also present. When Elizabeth brought the children into the room to bid their father farewell, Hamilton, the man who always had something to say, found it impossible to speak.[51] The image of his father lying motionless in a pool of blood on his death bed must have shocked the seven-year-old. His mother's wailing as she collapsed by his father's side may have remained etched in his memory for a long time.

Hamilton died on July 12, 1804. A full military-style funeral was held on July 14, 1804. People crowded to see the body of Hamilton for the last time. His four sons, Alexander, James, John, and William, headed the slow procession through the streets of New York City.[52] The sight of the broken and despondent children must have wrenched the hearts of the people. All work in the city stopped for the day as Hamilton's friends and even some of his enemies paid homage to the great statesman. Hamilton found his final resting place in the yard of the Old Trinity Church in New York City, the financial capital of the nation he had created and loved.

Hamilton's death added more responsibilities to Elizabeth's already-burdened shoulders. The family owed overwhelming obligations to creditors. In his will, Hamilton had asked his trustees to "sell all my Estate real and personal . . . to pay all debts that I shall owe at the time of my decease, in whole" and to pay any money left over "to my excellent and dear wife Elizabeth Hamilton." He had prayed to God that if there was an auction to pay off his debts, "something may remain for the maintenance and education of my dear wife and children."[53] For some time Elizabeth and the children survived on the generous support of friends and relatives, but things were difficult. William came of age during this precarious period of financial trouble for the Hamilton family.

Before his death, Hamilton had spent a considerable amount of time teaching his children.[54] He wanted them to have a chance to succeed in life, and he devoted the energy to mentor them whenever he could get away from his responsibilities at work. But the financial ruin and personal tragedy the family suffered after Hamilton's death interrupted William's formal education. Almost all of his elder brothers had completed their schooling at Columbia University or were on the verge of doing so. Unlike them, William was unable to attend the university. All his brothers, with the exception of Little Phil, joined the military after completing their education at Columbia. William also attended the US Military Academy at West Point, but he resigned, never to return, before completing the program in its entirety. No one knows why he left without completing his time at West Point. Perhaps the financial strain rendered him unable to continue. Or perhaps he decided to pursue other goals. The only thing certain is that he attended West Point from 1815 to 1817 and gained some knowledge about military training and operations before he left.[55]

According to William's elder brother John Church, as a young boy William attended school and "gathered knowledge without much labor."[56] Whether he remained in school long enough to complete his studies is uncertain. If we consider his record at West Point, the financial hardships confronted by his mother, and his brother John's assertions that William possessed a "courage[ous] and roving spirit," then it is possible that William learned whatever he could under the circumstances before he had to withdraw from school.

Although Hamilton's death left William without a large fortune, he did inherit his father's personal collection of books, including works by Jonathan Swift, Henry Fielding, Thomas Hobbes, Horace Walpole, Voltaire, William Robertson, Enticle, Edward Gibbon, Laurence Sterne, Thomas Rutherford, Socrates, Sir Thomas Browne, Saint Anselmo, Samuel Butler, Oliver Goldsmith, David Hume, Pliny, Cicero, Demosthenes, Francis Bacon, Ralt, Diderot, and Montaigne, among many others. In a letter written on April 1, 1880, to William's friend Cyrus Woodman, Edgar Hamilton confirmed that William received "law books, Voltaire and books in French" from his father.[57] William's friend and neighbor Henry Gratiot, who owned and operated Gratiot's Grove, a successful lead mining and smelting operation in Wisconsin, recalled seeing in Hamilton's cabin the "books of classical writers," a collection considered the "most valuable in the country."[58] Others visitors to William's home, such as Juliette Magill Kinzie— wife of William's friend John Kinzie (who was an Indian agent) and author of *Wau-Bun*, a book about Native American and pioneer relations in Wisconsin during the early nineteenth century—recalled seeing books. Even Rodolf, who was hardly a friend, remembered seeing some of the same collection.[59]

William may have remembered the training he received under the care of his father. Hamilton had written out a plan for Philip to follow that required him "to rise not later than Six Oclock—The rest of the year not later than Seven. If Earlier he will deserve commendation. Ten will be his hour of going to bed throughout the year." His day was to begin "from the time he is dressed in the morning till nine o clock (the time for breakfast Excepted)," when "he is to read Law. At nine he goes to the office & continues there till dinner time—he will be occupied partly in the writing and partly in reading law." Later in the afternoon, Philip could have dinner, then "reads law at home till five O clock." Thereafter, Philip was allowed some free time until "seven," and then he was required to read and study until "ten." On the weekends, "from twelve on Saturday he is at Liberty to amuse himself. On Sunday he will attend the morning Church. The rest of the day may be applied to innocent recreations." Hamilton enforced the strict regimen, emphasizing that Philip "must not Depart from any of these rules without my permission."[60] Hamilton may have suggested a similar schedule for William, who may have followed it to further his education even after his father's death. Regardless of how he obtained his education, William was more self-educated than any of his brothers.

As Elizabeth aged and the children grew older, the family dispersed, the members all trying to eke out a living for themselves. Without financial support from his father, it became crucial for William to grow up fast and find solid footing in the world. He did so by going to the frontier.

NOTES

1. Charles Stephenson to Cyrus Woodman, December 26, 1880, Woodman MSS. Stephenson interviewed William's friend Barney Norris, who was present when William fell ill and who visited him almost three times a day, every day, until William died. In 1880, on Woodman's request, Stephenson interviewed Norris about William's last hours and sent the information in writing to Woodman.

2. George Gratiot to Cyrus Woodman, April 8, 1880, Woodman MSS. George Gratiot met with the physician who had attended William during his illness. Dr. Crouin told Gratiot that William had suffered from a malarial fever that caused spinal exhaustion and paralysis and brought him great mental and physical strain prior to his death.

3. "Sacramento Transcript."

4. John C. Hamilton to Lyman Draper, September 24, 1855, Woodman MSS.

5. Harrison and Tilghman, "Image 90 of Memoir of Lieut. Col. Tench Tilghman."

6. Rodolf, "Pioneering in the Wisconsin Lead Region," 350.

7. Edgar Hamilton to Cyrus Woodman, June 2, 1880, Woodman MSS.

8. Edgar Hamilton, "Autobiography of Rev. Edgar A. Hamilton," 1.

9. Lord, *A Doctor's Gold Rush Journey to California*, 91.

10. Allan McLane Hamilton, *Intimate Life of Alexander Hamilton*, 222.

11. Edgar Hamilton to Cyrus Woodman, June 2, 1880, Woodman MSS.

12. Kinzie, *Wau-Bun*, 152.

13. Philip Hamilton to Cyrus Woodman, February 7, 1880, Woodman MSS.

14. Smith, *William S. Hamilton*.

15. Philip Hamilton to Cyrus Woodman, February 7, 1880, Woodman MSS.

16. Brookhiser, *Alexander Hamilton, American*, 16.

17. Chernow, *Alexander Hamilton*, 26.

18. Alexander Hamilton to Edward Stevens, November 11, 1769, in *Alexander Hamilton: Writings*, 3.

19. Chernow, *Alexander Hamilton*, 17, 33, 37.

20. John Adams to Abigail Adams, January 9, 1797, in *My Dearest Friend*, 424.

21. Chernow, *Alexander Hamilton*, 89.

22. Alexander Hamilton to John Laurens, ca. April 1779, in *Alexander Hamilton: Writings*, 58.

23. Allan McLane Hamilton, *Intimate Life of Alexander Hamilton*, 93.

24. Chernow, *Alexander Hamilton*, 130.

25. Gratiot, "Mrs. Gratiot's Narrative," 274. Adele Gratiot remembered that even though Elizabeth Hamilton Holly admonished her mother, Elizabeth Schuyler Hamilton loved going for long walks in the morning so she could pick wildflowers.

26. Alexander Hamilton to Elizabeth Schuyler, August 1780, in *Alexander Hamilton: Writings*, 66.

27. Chernow, *Alexander Hamilton*, 148.

28. Allan McLane Hamilton, *Intimate Life of Alexander Hamilton*, 210.

29. Alexander Hamilton to Richard Kidder Meade, August 27, 1782, in *Alexander Hamilton: Writings*, 119.

30. Alexander Hamilton to Philip Hamilton, December 5, 1791, in *Alexander Hamilton: Writings*, 735.

31. Chernow, *Alexander Hamilton*, 544–545.

32. Brookhiser, *Alexander Hamilton, American*, 198–199.

33. Alexander Hamilton to Benjamin Rush, March 29, 1802, in *Alexander Hamilton: Writings*, 987.

34. Alexander Hamilton to Angelica Hamilton, ca. November 1793, in *Alexander Hamilton: Writings*, 810.

35. Alexander Hamilton to William Hamilton, May 2, 1797, in *Alexander Hamilton: Writings*, 881.

36. James A. Hamilton, *Reminisces of James A. Hamilton*, 3.

37. Brookhiser, *Alexander Hamilton, American*, 200.

38. Alexander Hamilton to Charles Cotesworth Pinckney, December 29, 1802, in *Alexander Hamilton: Writings*, 994.

39. Philip Hamilton to Lyman C. Draper, February 7, 1880, Woodman MSS. According to William's great-nephew Edgar Hamilton, after Elizabeth Hamilton

Holly's death, her younger brother Philip Hamilton received all her property, including her letters to and from William. But Philip Hamilton stated that he never found any letters in his sister's belongings and that he believed she may have destroyed them.

40. Chernow, *Alexander Hamilton*, 726.

41. Allan McLane Hamilton, *Intimate Life of Alexander Hamilton*, 222.

42. Muldoon, *Alexander Hamilton's Pioneer Son*, 29.

43. Brookhiser, *Alexander Hamilton, American*, 204.

44. Chernow, *Alexander Hamilton*, 337, 643.

45. Allan McLane Hamilton, *Intimate Life of Alexander Hamilton*, 222.

46. Gratiot, "Mrs. Gratiot's Narrative," 274. Adele Gratiot wrote that Elizabeth Schuyler Hamilton spent almost three months on the frontier visiting with William and his friends and that she loved playing backgammon.

47. Allan McLane Hamilton, *Intimate Life of Alexander Hamilton*, 116–117.

48. Edgar A. Hamilton to Cyrus Woodman, January 23, 1880, Woodman MSS. Edgar Hamilton stated that the news of William's death was kept from his mother. Elizabeth Hamilton died four years after William in 1854, never knowing that her son was already dead.

49. Alexander Hamilton, "Alexander Hamilton, 'The Reynolds Pamphlet,'" in *Alexander Hamilton Writings*, 888.

50. Alexander Hamilton to Elizabeth Hamilton, July 4, 1804, in *Alexander Hamilton Writings*, 1019.

51. Chernow, *Alexander Hamilton*, 702.

52. Chernow, 713.

53. Alexander Hamilton, "Last Will and Testament of Alexander Hamilton, [9 July 1804]," Founders Online, National Archives, last modified April 12, 2018, https://founders.archives.gov/documents/Hamilton/01-26-02-0001-0259.

54. Chernow, *Alexander Hamilton*, 336.

55. Frank Micheu to Philip Hamilton, January 8, 1880, Woodman MSS.

56. John C. Hamilton to Lyman Draper, September 24, 1855, Woodman MSS.

57. Edgar A. Hamilton to Cyrus Woodman, April 1, 1880, Woodman MSS.

58. Charles Gratiot to Cyrus Woodman, February 23, 1880, Woodman MSS.

59. Kinzie, *Wau-Bun*, 150; Rodolf, "Pioneering in the Wisconsin Lead Region," 347.

60. Alexander Hamilton to Philip Hamilton, "Rules for Philip Hamilton," 1800, in *Alexander Hamilton Writings*, 932.

TWO

The Man

THE WESTERN FRONTIER DURING THE EARLY REPUBLIC was all land east of the Mississippi River. During this period of great change, Americans became more entrepreneurial as they created and sought opportunities for self-reliance and independence. New technology, industrialization, and land availability on the frontier allowed average Americans to move beyond the eastern states and work toward improving their own future. By 1787, the Northwest Ordinance had opened the area in the southern Great Lakes region for settlement. People arrived from Virginia, Pennsylvania, and New York in boats, in wagons, on horses, and even on foot. By the first decade of the nineteenth century, one-third of Americans from the eastern states were already living in the area. The ordinance gave the federal government control of the territory and marked the manner in which new states could gain admission to the Union and thereby avoid any conflict with foreigners. Nonetheless, the leaders back on the East Coast became nervous about people living on the frontier. They feared that the settlers would leave the union and join other nations.[1] Both Britain and Spain hunkered beyond the southern and western boundaries.

At the conclusion of the War of 1812, many Americans on the East Coast found themselves unemployed, owing high taxes, and owning no property. The war had decreased the need for American-produced goods in Europe, causing many hardships for Americans. Furthermore, even though the country remained agriculturally based, times were changing, and the younger generation of Americans diverged from the traditional roles. Gone were the days when sons worked and stayed close to the family home. Young men wanted to own land and start their own families. Others craved excitement and adventure, and the untamed frontier beckoned. In 1815, the Great Migration marked the westward movement for many Americans looking to escape the difficult conditions prevalent on the East Coast, and William, like many others, chose to make his fortune on the frontier.

Becoming a land surveyor was one way a young man could gain a foothold in the new territory. The Act of April 29, 1816, chapter 151, created the position of surveyor general in the territory of Illinois, Missouri, and Arkansas, with William C. Rector, from Perry County, Indiana, in charge. Born in 1773, Rector became an influential surveyor and renowned frontiersman. He surveyed the Third Principal Meridian in late 1805, and by 1816 he had garnered enough respect for his work to be appointed surveyor general by Josiah Meigs, commissioner of the Government Land Office.[2]

Surveying was a hard and confusing profession during the early Republic. With squatters, Native American cessions, new regulations, and minimal training, land surveys often resulted in either incomplete work or marked errors. The untamed frontier was a challenge with its unexpected waterways, harsh weather conditions, and lack of roads.

Furthermore, the government paid surveyors low wages for hard work that often required living in the wilderness, making the profession even less appealing to those with a genteel upbringing. Rector began hiring deputy surveyors, offering them just enough money to get by. William, who probably acquired some knowledge of surveying when he was at West Point, applied for the job. His contract with the government, dated May 17, 1820, stated it would pay "to the said William S. Hamilton, on account of the United States, as a full compensation for the whole expense of surveying, making the plats, descriptions and aforesaid, Three Dollars per mile for every mile and part of a mile that shall be actually surveyed and marked (random lines and offsets not included) provided no member of congress have any part in this contract."[3]

In addition to receiving low wages, surveyors also had to pay for their own expenses up front. They often hired a team that included chainmen and axmen. The surveyor ran the line, the axmen cleared the pathway, and the chainmen measured the distance surveyed. In addition to paying the hired help, surveyors purchased their own equipment, which included surveying instruments, chains, books, writing tools, and compasses. They often lived with the bare necessities, including just a tent, blankets, and some cooking utensils. Their rations were made up of flour, pork, beans, tea, coffee, and salt. Yet, with all its shortcomings, surveying was considered a respectable profession.[4] Surveying allowed William to learn a craft from self-study and hands-on experience, things he had practiced since his youth. It also gave him the chance to establish himself on the frontier.

William preferred wearing frontier clothing. Most frontiersmen wore a beaver hat, a linen hunting shirt, buckskin leggings over trousers, and a pair of well-worn boots. Juliette Kinzie noted that when she first met William in the Midwest, her "laughing" husband informed her that "Mr. William hesitated to present himself" in front of her because he was "unwilling" to allow her to see him "in his present mode of life."[5] Even later in life, William's habit of dressing casually remained. As late as 1850, Dr. Lord recorded in his journal that William's "exterior is now not of the smoothest, though a decent hat would much improve it. He is wearing or rather is capped with, an old rusty, torn, shockingly dilapidated, part of a straw hat—the major part it is true but a very considerable minority has seceded."[6] But despite his shabby wardrobe, which was drawn mainly on the basic necessities for survival on the frontier, William did own several linen shirts and a fancier blue coat, which he wore when he felt it was necessary.[7]

At least one historian has placed William arriving in Illinois in 1817 and living in Springfield.[8] Muldoon wrote that William came to

Missouri just before he turned nineteen (which would put his arrival there in 1815) and lived in Saint Louis before moving to Illinois.[9] Both dates present their own set of challenges. William was attending West Point in 1815. And on August 1, 1819, William wrote from Saint Louis to his family in New York about the "State of Illinois which is to be my future place of residence."[10]

As to living in Springfield in 1817, William resigned from West Point in September of that year and could have relocated to the Midwest that fall. But he must have been living in Saint Louis to have contracted to work for Rector, who had his headquarters in that city at the time.[11] As of November 1, 1819, he had also signed up as a subscriber "for the establishment of an Episcopal Church in St. Louis."[12] Furthermore, although a few squatters had built log cabins by the time Illinois was admitted to the Union in 1818, the area only had thirty-three counties, and neither Springfield nor Sangamon County existed. Sangamon County was formed in 1821: the first public survey was conducted that year, and the first land sale was recorded in 1823. When the first plat for Springfield was laid out in 1822, the area was named Calhoun after Senator John C. Calhoun of South Carolina.[13]

On the other hand, at that time Saint Louis had doubled its population since the switch from French to American control. Approximately five thousand people were living in town. Buildings reflecting American taste stood beside the old French architecture. Printing, banking, military-service, and steamboat businesses opened up, even as fur trading continued to be a part of the growing economy. Evidence suggests that William probably lived in St. Louis until about the time Sangamon County in Illinois was established.

In 1820 William had signed a contract to "lay off and survey the entire boundary lines and also subdivide into sections and establish corners for quarter sections the following described Townships of Land." The provisions of the contract gave specific instructions to "complete the surveys, plats and descriptions and calculations as aforesaid, and make return thereof together with the field notes to the Office of the Surveyor of the Lands of the United States for the State of Illinois & Territory of Missouri & Arkansas within six months from the date hereof." The contract also listed the penalty for failure of performance: "And that, on penalty of forfeiture and paying to the United States the sum of One Thousand Dollars if default be made on any of the foregoing conditions."[14] Then in 1821, William enrolled himself as a member of the Saint Louis bar, indicating that he may still have been living there.[15] Lawyers commonly rode the circuit and traveled from Saint Louis to Illinois and surrounding states to earn a living, and William may have done the same.[16] His earliest known appearance in a Sangamon County court was in 1824 or 1825.[17] Therefore, it seems that William first moved to the area that later became Springfield in 1820 or 1821 as a land surveyor, a lawyer, or both.

Although William seems to have left New York for the Midwest to improve his future, other possibilities require further consideration. Muldoon quotes historian John Berry as stating that after mortally wounding Hamilton, Burr ran off to Saint Louis. William soon followed and challenged him to a duel to avenge his father's murder, but Burr declined because of William's "youth and his own old age."[18] Another historian has also given credence to the supposed duel challenge.[19] Edgar Hamilton refuted the tale in 1880, stating that Mrs. Hamilton had required all of her sons to "promise" they would never engage in dueling and that "William S. Hamilton loved his mother too dearly to violate his promise."[20] Yet even if William was unable to keep his promise to his mother, he was a mere nine-year-old boy who could not have made a long journey alone to challenge a grown man to a duel in 1805 or 1806—which was the last time Burr is known to have visited Saint Louis.

Another incentive for William's move to the frontier may have been tension at home. William shunned the refinements of high-class society and "was ill at ease with the forms and ceremonies of a polite life" that may have been important to other members of his family.[21] Edgar Hamilton wrote that William "was entirely unconventional in fact had so identified himself with the rude conditions of that early western life" and "that his manners were criticized in the courtly home of his brother James."[22] After William's death, Edgar

Hamilton regretted that "his family who were abundantly able" had not erected a tombstone on his grave and "[had] left this work to a friend."[23] Charles Stephenson, William's friend and neighbor, voiced the same concern: "I feel ashamed of his mean brothers. Who are men of wealth, to think they could perish one of the family to be buried, in an unknown grave all these long years without a stone to mark the spot."[24] Although the suggestion that he may have been at odds with some of his family members was disturbing to Stephenson, it may explain William's hesitation to remain in New York.

William and his sister Eliza shared many letters, and after her death in 1857, her younger brother Philip acquired all her papers.[25] Philip later claimed that Eliza "must have destroyed her letters" and that he had "not recd papers or letter relating to, or from William to his mother, or brothers or any one."[26] Although Philip provided Woodman with details about William, the information he sent only skimmed the surface. He did not mention much of William's life in the Midwest, perhaps indicating that he preferred to leave some things unmentioned or was unaware of his brother's life away from New York.

Muldoon has noted that when William was living in Wisconsin, some of the brothers were unhappy with his decision to allow a female member of the family to live in his home.[27] Who was this female member of the Hamilton family who may have caused such a turn of events? What was her relationship to William? Muldoon did not explore these questions deeply, but further exploration may yield a better understanding of the cause of such an awkward situation.

Born in 1816 to Captain John Romer and Leah Van Tassel Romer, Angeline Romer was twenty-two years old when she married John Cornelius Adrian Hamilton, one of William's nephews and a son of John Church Hamilton. Angeline's father was a Revolutionary War veteran, and her mother was a descendant of Katrina Van Tassel, made famous in Washington Irving's "The Legend of Sleepy Hollow."[28] Angeline was a dark-haired beauty with deep-set eyes, and she was four years older than John Cornelius. He stood at five foot ten, had dark hair, and was completely smitten by her beauty. Neither their age nor the differences in their upbringing seem to have been of any consequence to the lovebirds.

Before meeting Angeline, John Cornelius attended Princeton. John Church may have heard rumors about his son's poor habits in college and decided that an overseas voyage to China would benefit John Cornelius's future prospects. John Cornelius seems to have gone on a three-year trip to China without much argument. On his return, he became "an assistant Engineer of the Croton Aqueduct." He also met Angeline in New York, the two fell in love and decided to get married on September 13, 1838. John Church appears to have been displeased with the match, but he was unable to stop the wedding. Perhaps too embarrassed to introduce his new daughter-in-law to his friends in the New York elite society, John Church sent John Cornelius and Angeline West with promises of giving them "property and abundance." Never one who could stand up to his father, John Cornelius took his new bride to the frontier, traveling from New York to Springfield, Illinois, where he worked as an engineer until August 19, 1839.[29]

It was in Springfield on August 1, 1839, that Angeline gave birth to their firstborn son. They named the baby William Stephen Hamilton, after his great-uncle. Sometime in 1839–1840, John Cornelius took his family to live in Wiota at Hamilton's Diggings. In 1841, the couple had their second child, named Edgar Augustus Hamilton. William tried to persuade John Cornelius to take up the study of law to support his growing family.[30] The object was never pursued by John Cornelius with any gravity. William then tried to get work for John Cornelius as a surveyor, but it is unknown what became of the opportunity.[31] By 1842, Angeline was pregnant with their third child, John Cornelius Leon Hamilton. That year, tragedy struck the young family: Baby William died after his third birthday.[32]

Whether or not John Cornelius was living up to his parents' expectations before his marriage is anyone's guess; however, letters shared between him and his family in New York between 1842 and 1845 show a growing rift between the parties. A letter from E. W. Turner, an acquaintance from Galena, Illinois, written on May 19, 1842, indicates that John Church was concerned about "conflicting statements" he had heard about his son's behavior.[33] Turner followed up with another letter in June that notified John Church that he had "made strict inquiry with regards to the unfavorable news you had of [John Cornelius] and find it only partially confirmed" and that "his uncle William has been ... more than he has for any slight deviation from morality which he may have been guilty of as well as the society he has been forced into at his present place of residence—Wiota." He reassured John Church that if his son purchased farmland and settled in Galena instead, he would "have no such opportunity" unless "he forces himself in it," which "from his appearance and everything else, he has no inclination to do."[34] In other words, living in Wiota, under William's roof, may have worsened John Cornelius's behavior if he was already immoral or had allowed him to pick up some bad habits because of the company he kept under William's charge.

It is also evident that there was some strain in the marriage between John Cornelius and Angeline. In his June letter, Turner told John Church that Angeline was in Galena with her husband and their children and "intended on leaving yesterday morning with her children for her father's residency" back in New York. However, he offered some reassurance: "But I believe I have succeeded in persuading her to remain until your son and myself can hear from you again."[35] She was pregnant, he was keeping bad company, and they were far away from home. In 1844, John Cornelius confessed his guilt in a heart-wrenching letter to his mother, Maria Eliza Van den Heuvel Hamilton: "I have one regret and that is my family. By them I have acted wrongfully."[36]

If John Cornelius's relationship with his wife was strained, his relationship with his father became a hopeless issue. The young man who had once gone overseas to appease his father now asked his father to support his endeavors, but John Church was beyond frustrated with his son's repeated mistakes. He told his son, "You have violated every assurance you have made and no confidence can be placed in your statements." He offered John Cornelius twenty dollars to start over at Prairie du Chien with a warning that "I am resolved to do nothing else" and that "I shall neither provide for you, nor give myself any further trouble about you."[37] John Cornelius did not settle in Prairie du Chien as his father may have ordered. He did, however, obey his father's wish and removed himself to Marshall, Michigan, walking fifty miles from Galena, Illinois.[38] Once in Marshall, he tried to start a business venture in selling paints, but that too was a short-lived dream.[39] On March 6, 1847, in New Orleans, John Cornelius enlisted in the US Army to serve in the Mexican-American War, but he seems to have deserted less than five months later. Thereafter, he continued to wander from one place to the next until reaching California, where he remained until his death. Years later, Edgar Hamilton wrote, "His natural weakness of will was overcome by fear of his father and careless habits led to that manner of life which ended so unhappily for his own family, himself and my mother and her children."[40] John Cornelius died in 1879 and was buried in Merced, California. John Cornelius was never reunited with Angeline or their children.

On the evening of May 10, 1856, a young boy carried a letter to John Church Hamilton's residence in New York. When asked, the boy "said he did not know the person who gave it to him," only that it "was a gentleman at the Astor House." The letter was signed by Monroe Alexander and came as a warning that "unless immediately attended to will cause you mortification and trouble and perhaps cast disgrace upon your family." The writer continued, "I will briefly state the matter, I suppose you are aware although possibly you may not be that your son John is a bigamist. That at this very moment he has two wives living." The accuser was certain that John Cornelius "by his acts and wiles, by passing himself off as a single man" had "won the affections of this lady and married her." Furthermore, "in less than a fortnight finding his liberty in danger he left her." Now the said lady wanted to "lead a life of usefulness and virtue" and "she asks, nay demands your aid." What aid did she demand? She wanted $500 "with which she will return to the west and set up the business of a milliner or dress maker." Of course John Church should consider the matter with all seriousness, "or else consequences may be . . . dreadful." In the event that John Church was skeptical, "an interview with this daughter-in-law" could be arranged.[41]

John Church made no reply to the letter. Four days later, he received
another note around 9:00 p.m. from the same Monroe Alexander.
The writer stated that the lady's "necessities" had led her to "demand
your assistance"; otherwise, "she desires to injure no one." He added
a threat that if John Church ignored the "suffering to which she has
been resigned by your son she will feel resentful—she will avenge
herself upon your family." Matters would be brought out in the open,
and she would "bring your son to justice. You may think him secure
because away, but Sir, he is within reach." As if to emphasize the point,
the letter added that the lady had already paid a visit to Angeline
"residing in Westchester County without disclosing who she was."
In response, John Church warned the delivery boy and "ordered him
never to bring another note." The matter was dropped, and no other
note is known to have arrived.[42]

When Angeline lived with her family in William's home, she was
treated with respect and kindness. Edgar Hamilton wrote that "his
kindness to them, especially to my mother was a theme she never
tired to tell to my brother and myself when young" and he "always
looked upon my father and mother and we babies as his special heirs
and expected to educate us and leave his property to us."[43] William's
generosity and protection extended to Angeline and her children
even in John Cornelius's absence. She, for her part, took care of his
home, even making suits and linen shirts that he later wore to the
legislative sessions in Madison, Wisconsin. By 1843, the loss of a child,
stress in her marriage, and news of an ailing father all prompted Angeline to consider going back to New York. William, who at the time
was running for elected office and hoped to become the new governor
of the territory, had asked Angeline to put off her journey until after
the election. But she took her children and went home to be with her
father. William always considered them his family, and in his last letter to Angeline, he wished that she and her children, along with his
then widowed sister Eliza, would join him and become a part of his
household.[44]

Until the end of her life, Angeline held the deepest respect for
William and considered him her "truest friend in the family."[45] If

any romantic involvement between William and Angeline may have caused a strain between William and his brothers, no such evidence exists in primary sources. Moreover, Edgar Hamilton wrote that Angeline "still retained a warm love for her husband and esteem for his many admirable qualities. Though opportunities of marriage came to her afterwards, it was his memory which held her true to her early vows and made her the noble woman and devoted mother."[46] The most that can be said about their relationship based on evidence is that each had a deep level of respect, care, and admiration for the other.

Angeline stayed with her father and children in New York until the beginning of the Civil War. Thereafter, she relocated to Missouri with her son Edgar and lived in Springfield until her death in 1889.[47] Angeline never remarried.

As he had helped John Cornelius and Angeline Hamilton with their young family during a time of great need, William also cared for others who were helpless. Edgar Hamilton wrote that William "as a leader" was "a man of indomitable will, generous to a fault, [and] hospitable."[48] He remained a friend to the downtrodden, and "his feelings always were quickened in behalf of the poor or distressed ladies."[49] When Kinzie and his wife were lost in the woods, they were grateful to find refuge in William's home: "Every spot was solitary and deserted; not even the trace of a recent fire, to cheer us with the hope of human beings within miles of us. Suddenly, a shout from the foremost of the party made each heart bound with joy. 'Une clôture! une clôture!' (A fence! a fence!) It was almost like life to the dead." The fence belonged to William's house, and the Kinzies found it a "most welcome shelter from the pelting storm."[50]

In another incident when William was riding his sleigh, he "interfered" when he saw a Native American man beating his wife. He then took the woman "in the sleigh" and tried to remove her from immediate danger. The man followed William and tried to shoot him but missed his mark. William turned around and gave the man a "tremendous thrashing with his Horse whip" before taking off in his sleigh.[51]

During the time he lived in the Midwest, William owned at least one sleigh for transportation and perhaps even for sport. His mother had presented him with a gift of sleigh bells, two of which remain in the Wisconsin Historical Society's collections. The bells are large and made of solid brass. Age has brought faint cracks and slight discoloration around some edges, but the bells still ring loud and clear, as if their owner is riding the sleigh and will appear around the corner at any moment. The same bells may have been on the sleigh during the incident with the Native American couple.

Despite his feelings about upper-class conventions and formalities, William was "always cordial and genial and frank in his manners towards all."[52] His friends held him in high esteem for "his warm social instincts, his affability, his unassumed courteousness, his refinement and culture" and described him as "warm, temperate and generous to a fault."[53] Others found him to be a "brave, generous, hospitable and humane" individual who was "usually quick in perception and decided in action."[54] In 1870, Christina Holmes Tillson, wife of influential Illinois merchant John Tillson, remembered William as among her "acquaintances and personal friends" and felt that the "recollection of our friendly intercourse is to me a source of enjoyment."[55] Stephenson called him a "generous hearted little man" and "brilliant."[56] Even Rodolf, who otherwise found William to be more or less a backwoodsman, noted that he was a man of "culture" who could show his polished manners when he desired it.[57]

Multiple accounts indicate that William had a soft spot for the ladies. Considering the rough frontier society he lived in, it is possible that he was involved in a tryst or two himself. Yet it is difficult to ascertain whether any such interludes left him yearning for matrimony, because he left no records on the subject. Did he prefer his freedom? Was he spurned by someone? Did he recall his father's adultery and the shame it had brought on the whole family? Without concrete evidence, it is difficult to prove any given theory. One can only conclude that if there was a special romance, William chose not to pursue it and remained a bachelor all his life.

Romantic notions aside, William held a deep regard for the women in his life, as is obvious from his close attachment to his mother and to his sister Eliza. The brother and sister "wrote regularly to each other from the time he went west." She was his "favorite sister. He loved her. And her sympathies were true and strong and devoted to him."[58] Following the death of his sister's husband in 1842, William intended to bring her to the Midwest to live with him.[59]

His concern for his mother in particular remained paramount until the end. One of the few surviving letters of William from 1848, two years prior to his death, shows his eagerness to assure his mother of his well-being. He begs his friend, Wisconsin politician John H. Tweedy, to visit her: "My mother is in Washington you will confer a favor upon me by calling and introducing yourself to her as a friend of mine it will give her great pleasure." In February of the same year, he asked if Tweedy had "seen [his] mother as requested."[60] It seems that the extended separation from both his mother and sister was a struggle for William.

All the accounts thus far have helped create an image of a generous, kind, and loyal man—a sharp contrast to Rodolf's view of William as a "gambler and a libertine."[61] Even William's friend Stephenson admitted that William "easily partook of the vices of the country," possibly referring to drinking and gambling, because "his nature and character were such that he could not help it."[62] Edgar Hamilton wrote that William "was prodigal of his resources according to the manners of that day" and that "he would accumulate his tens of thousands of dollars in the summer and then with companies of gentlemen would squander it in winter by sailing down the Mississippi River and playing cards."[63] Others described him as "a man of great intellectual powers, but . . . unsteady in his habits."[64] Most damning of all, his political rivals tagged him as "the little scion of a great family."[65] So, which description of William is accurate? Two of his political rivals, Cyrus Woodman and Henry Dodge, offer the best testimony to William's personality and traits.

Woodman graduated from Bowdoin College and Harvard Law School and practiced law in Boston before arriving in the Midwest in 1840. He forged a successful partnership with Cadwallader Colden Washburne—who later became governor of Wisconsin—in a land, law, and banking business for eleven years. By the time he retired to his family home in Cambridge, Massachusetts, Woodman was quite wealthy, and he remained a distinguished gentleman until his death in 1889. Although Woodman opposed William's political stand, he did not allow party politics to get in the way of common decency and friendship. He spent a considerable amount of time, energy, and money to locate bits of information regarding William's death. Indeed, most primary sources discussing William appear in the archives of the Woodman Papers in the Wisconsin Historical Society collections.

Woodman wrote letters to William's friends, relatives, neighbors, acquaintances, and even political rivals asking about his last days in an effort to find his remains. In one instance, when writing to Henry Dodge, Woodman's tone was gruff: "Hamilton, howmuchsoever we may differ with him in some of his political theories, was, undeniably, a great man and a genuine patriot. He served his country faithfully and well, and so commands the gratitude of every true American."[66] In response to another letter, he received a reply from Edgar Hamilton, expressing his thanks: "The kindness of your feeling with the proofs of your sincere regard for the memory of my great uncle William Stephen Hamilton has called out toward you a sense of obligation and gratitude."[67] William's sister, Eliza, shared Woodman's letter with her brothers and then wrote back to him "to express with the deepest emotion their and my acknowledgment for the friendly interest you evince in our brother's memory."[68] Stephenson responded, "But for your care, kindness and attention, his body would now rest in an unknown grave." He felt that Woodman "should have many marks to [his] credit for the many generous acts of this kind [he had] performed," and he expressed his own thanks: "In this instance I feel very grateful myself for what you have done. I thank you from the bottom of my heart."[69] Woodman was so keen on ensuring that William would receive a respectful burial that even after an interval of more than twenty years, he made sure William's grave was found and a marker placed on it indicating William's final resting place.

It can be argued that Woodman was trying to make a good impression on his contemporaries. Considering that Woodman was not obligated to William for any special reason, his efforts to locate William's remains probably came from a simple motive: friendship. Despite their political differences, Woodman held William in the highest regard and worked with vigor to give him a proper place in American history.

Unlike Woodman, Henry Dodge and William had shared heated words on more than one occasion. Aside from their political differences, Dodge being a staunch Democrat and William being a Whig, both men lived and worked in the same lead region. It was inevitable that they would clash in a frontier society where every man was trying to accomplish something, especially an honorable reputation.

Born in Vincennes in what is now the state of Indiana, Dodge arrived in Wisconsin in 1827. He was the first governor of the Territory of Wisconsin, a delegate to Congress from the Territory of Wisconsin, and a US senator from Wisconsin. He and William had both participated in the Winnebago War of 1827 and the Black Hawk War of 1832. During the Black Hawk War, Dodge challenged William to a duel over what he felt was disobedience of direct orders on William's part. Dodge "stopped his horse, and, as Hamilton approached, sprang off, and presented Hamilton with the butt ends of his two pistols, and entreated him to take choice, that the question might be settled there and then which was to be commander." One source reports that William refused to take the bait and rebuffed Dodge's challenge to a duel.[70] In 1879, another of William's nephews, Schuyler Hamilton, wrote about quite possibly the same incident, stating that William responded to Dodge's challenge by saying that "if he survived until the war was over he would be happy to oblige him." Yet, after the war, Dodge recanted his challenge because "he could have no cause of quarrel with so brave a soldier and gentleman as he had shown himself" and the men became friends.[71] Dodge's son A. C., who had spent time under William's command during the Winnebago War, noted that even though his father and William "had some unpleasant personal difficulties, ephemeral in their nature, my brother, sister & self were always on excellent terms with Hamilton." Whatever his father's sentiments toward William, Dodge's son thought William "was one of the most interesting & clever of Wisconsin Pioneers & in many respects a remarkable and meritorious man."[72]

Life on the frontier was rough, but in its own way, the untamed frontier was also beautiful. Similarly, William, who lived a hard life among rough people, maintained a sense of consideration and care toward others. Whatever vices he may have had did not stop him from gaining loyal friends, and even respect from his foes. In this, William was much the same as us: a complicated, multifaceted, and imperfect human being.

NOTES

1. Wood, *Idea of America*, 269.
2. Morrow, "Surveyor's Challenges."
3. William Stephen Hamilton, "Contracts with Surveyors," 1820.
4. Buley, *Old Northwest Pioneer Period*, 119, 122.
5. Kinzie, *Wau-Bun*, 148.
6. Lord, *A Doctor's Gold Rush Journey to California*, 91.
7. Edgar Hamilton to Cyrus Woodman, June 2, 1880, Woodman MSS.
8. Gara, "William S. Hamilton on the Wisconsin Frontier," 25.
9. Muldoon, *Alexander Hamilton's Pioneer Son*, 33.
10. William Stephen Hamilton to John C. Hamilton, August 1, 1819, Woodman MSS.
11. White, *History of the Rectangular Survey System*, 72.
12. Houck, *History of Missouri*, 234–235.
13. Power, *History of Springfield, Illinois*, 10.
14. William Stephen Hamilton, "Contracts with Surveyors," 1820.
15. "Early Lawyers of St. Louis," June 10, 1894.
16. Chroust, "Legal Profession in Early Missouri," 3.
17. Palmer, *Bench and Bar of Illinois*, 159.
18. Muldoon, *Alexander Hamilton's Pioneer Son*, 34. Muldoon refers to an article by historian J. Berry titled "The Hamiltons," which appeared in the *Freeman* newspaper on April 17, 1880, and which describes the exchange between William and Aaron Burr. Muldoon says he is unsure whether the story is true, but he believes it to be a "fact" true to William's character.
19. Rennick, "Peoria and Galena Trail," 419. Rennick's article was published in 1908, years before Muldoon's biography. Like Muldoon, Rennick may have used

Berry as his source. He too states that there is some truth to the story but does not provide any evidence for the assertion. The article "The Hamiltons," written by Berry in the *Peoria Freeman* in 1880 and quoted by others, does not provide any evidence of the duel but supposes it to be a true account.

20. Edgar Hamilton to Cyrus Woodman, June 2, 1880, Woodman MSS.

21. Edgar Hamilton to Cyrus Woodman, box 1, Woodman MSS.

22. Edgar Hamilton, "Autobiography of Rev. Edgar A. Hamilton," 1.

23. Edgar Hamilton to Cyrus Woodman, January 13, 1880, Woodman MSS.

24. Charles Stephenson to Cyrus Woodman, January 8, 1880, Woodman MSS.

25. Edgar Hamilton to Cyrus Woodman, January 23, 1880, Woodman MSS.

26. Philip Hamilton to Cyrus Woodman, February 7, 1880, Woodman MSS.

27. Muldoon, *Alexander Hamilton's Pioneer Son*, 142.

28. Reynolds, *Genealogical and Family History of Southern New York and the Hudson River Valley*, 1386.

29. John Cornelius Adrian Hamilton to Maria Eliza Van den Heuvel Hamilton, September 8, 1839, private collection of Douglas Hamilton.

30. John Cornelius Adrian Hamilton to Maria Eliza Van den Heuvel Hamilton, March 1, 1841, private collection of Douglas Hamilton.

31. John Cornelius Adrian Hamilton to Maria Eliza Van den Heuvel Hamilton, November 8, 1841, private collection of Douglas Hamilton.

32. John Cornelius Adrian Hamilton to Maria Eliza Van den Heuvel Hamilton, September 5, 1842, private collection of Douglas Hamilton.

33. E. W. Turner to John C. Hamilton, May 19, 1842, Hamilton Family MSS.

34. E. W. Turner to John C. Hamilton, June 11, 1842, Hamilton Family MSS.

35. E. W. Turner to John C. Hamilton, June 11, 1842, Hamilton Family MSS.

36. John Cornelius Adrian Hamilton to Maria Eliza Van den Heuvel Hamilton, January 1844, Hamilton Family MSS.

37. John C. Hamilton to John Cornelius Adrian Hamilton, August 8, 1845, Hamilton Family MSS.

38. John Cornelius Adrian Hamilton to Maria Eliza Van den Heuvel Hamilton, March 30, 1843, private collection of Douglas Hamilton.

39. M. Callender to John Church Hamilton, August 16, 1843, private collection of Douglas Hamilton.

40. Edgar Hamilton, "Autobiography of Rev. Edgar Hamilton," 3.

41. Monroe Alexander to John C. Hamilton, May 10, 1856, Hamilton Family MSS.

42. Monroe Alexander to John C. Hamilton, May 14, 1856, Hamilton Family MSS.

43. Edgar Hamilton, "Autobiography of Rev. Edgar A. Hamilton," 1–2.

44. Edgar Hamilton to Cyrus Woodman, June 2, 1880, Woodman MSS.

45. Edgar Hamilton to Cyrus Woodman, January 23, 1880, Woodman MSS.

46. Edgar Hamilton, "Autobiography of Rev. Edgar A. Hamilton," 3–4.

47. Edgar Hamilton to Cyrus Woodman, box 1, Woodman MSS.

48. Edgar Hamilton, "Autobiography of Rev. Edgar A. Hamilton," 1.

49. Edgar Hamilton to Cyrus Woodman, June 2, 1880, Woodman MSS.

50. Kinzie, *Wau-Bun*, 146.

51. Edgar Hamilton to Cyrus Woodman, box 1, Woodman MSS.

52. Edgar Hamilton to Cyrus Woodman, June 2, 1880, Woodman MSS.

53. Charles Gratiot to Cyrus Woodman, February 23, 1880, Woodman MSS.

54. Washburne, *Sketch of Edward Coles*, 189.

55. Tillson, *Woman's Story of Pioneer Illinois*, 7–8.

56. Charles Stephenson to Cyrus Woodman, January 8, 1880, Woodman MSS.

57. Rodolf, "Pioneering in the Wisconsin Lead Region," 350.

58. Edgar A. Hamilton to Cyrus Woodman, January 23, 1880, Woodman MSS.

59. Edgar A. Hamilton to Cyrus Woodman, box 1, Woodman MSS.

60. William Stephen Hamilton to John Hubbard Tweedy, January and February 1848, boxes 1 and 2, Tweedy MSS.

61. Theodore Rodolf to Cyrus Woodman, April 15, 1880, Woodman MSS.

62. Charles Stephenson to Cyrus Woodman, January 8, 1880, Woodman MSS.

63. Edgar Hamilton, "Autobiography of Rev. Edgar Hamilton," 2.

64. Palmer, *Bench and Bar of Illinois*, 159.

65. Schafer, *Wisconsin Lead Region*, 53.

66. Cyrus Woodman to Henry Dodge, June 28, 1851, Woodman MSS.

67. Edgar Hamilton to Cyrus Woodman, January 23, 1880, Woodman MSS.

68. Eliza Hamilton to Cyrus Woodman, February 13, 1856, Woodman MSS.

69. Charles Stephenson to Cyrus Woodman, January 8, 1880, Woodman MSS.

70. Salter, *Life of Henry Dodge*, 44–45.

71. Schuyler Hamilton to L. C. Draper, June 14, 1879, Woodman MSS.

72. A. C. Dodge to Cyrus Woodman, July 3, 1833, Woodman MSS.

THREE

Life in Illinois

BY THE 1820S THE UNITED STATES WAS CHANGING FROM AN international trade economy to a national market economy. Americans were relying less on selling their goods to European markets and were focusing on manufacturing wares for their neighboring states. National systems of transportation and communication made trade within the nation possible. Americans took advantage of various opportunities in manufacturing goods to improve their economic condition.

A promissory note William wrote on August 10, 1825, for $350 to pay someone named Edward Dick Taylor by April 1826 shows he was still struggling financially and had to borrow funds to survive.[1] At this stage in his life, William was trying any type of work to establish himself. As early as 1819, William had shown an interest in politics and shared his sentiments with his brother: "The fact is our Society come under Loch Ideas of Natural Liberty as existing among a Civilized Community it produces [unclear word] anarchy and not Liberty for the strong have the advantage of the weak and the Dishonorable man the superiority of the honorable."[2] By 1824, William was running for political office in Illinois. He won the election and became the representative from Sangamon County, holding the same seat later occupied by Abraham Lincoln in 1834.[3] As a legislator, William "introduced a new road law, which passed the legislature." The new law, requiring people to pay a tax for road construction and repairs, replaced one that only asked every able-bodied man to work five days each year on building or repairing the roads. Within the year, the 1825 law was repealed because it received too much opposition from people who preferred to work on the roads rather than to pay taxes for it.[4]

William still worked as a US surveyor during this period. In 1823, he had surveyed lots of land near the Illinois River for French settlers who had made claims to the land.[5] On July 10, 1826, he surveyed what became the town of Peoria and platted its streets. The county commissioner's office paid him $58.95 for his work, "for which he [had] agreed to receive two town lots" as full payment.[6]

William also worked as a lawyer in Peoria, and in 1825 he defended a Native American man named Nom-A-Que in the first murder trial held in town.[7] Nom-A-Que was a Potawatomi man, "tall in stature, muscular and a hunter," who had arrived at a fur-trading post in Peoria in September with the intention to stay. But Nom-A-Que's plans were short-lived, as weeks later he was charged with stabbing and murdering a Frenchman named Pierre Laundri "with a scalping knife during a drunken brawl." The court tried Nom-A-Que, found him guilty, and convicted him to death by hanging. William appealed the case to the Supreme Court of Illinois, the first such case to be appealed in the history of Peoria. The case was "remanded back for another trial."

Nom-A-Que was retried in October 1826. He was found guilty again, and the death penalty remained in effect. At this point, William changed tactics and argued that "the court did not have jurisdiction" to try Nom-A-Que for a crime because he was a member of the Potawatomi tribe and was only "so far bound by the laws of the State of Illinois as his tribe had made him by treaty." Thus, William asked the court to dismiss the case against Nom-A-Que. On May 15, 1828, the court agreed with William's petition and Nom-A-Que was released. Years later, Nom-A-Que reappeared in the Black Hawk War opposite William and the US military. He was killed in action at the Battle of Stillman's Run.[8]

When the US military needed someone to drive cattle from Illinois to Fort Howard at Green Bay in 1825, William agreed to the conditions and signed the contract. He paid about ten dollars per head for almost seven hundred cattle to be transported to the Mackinaw. It is possible that he hired four men to make the delivery for him but decided to accompany them himself when he found them feeling "discouraged" because they had lost one of the drovers. He left from Springfield, picked up the herd by the Mackinaw, and drove them north toward Green Bay, passing through the Illinois River on to Chicago. He traveled through uncharted territory, crossing dangerous wilderness and waterways, risking possible stampedes and Native American attacks. He stopped at Chicago, where he met some men from the American Fur Company and the US military. When he resumed his journey, he stayed close to Lake Michigan and passed first Grosse Pointe, then Milwaukee. In Milwaukee, he found a "starved out" man named Solomon Juneau who was thrilled "to see him and his provisions." Leaving Milwaukee, William passed through Manitowoc and broke off from Lake Michigan, arriving at Fort Howard a week ahead of schedule. He made the entire trip without losing any cattle except one that was drowned by a man in Chicago (so that he could purchase it from William, who would have otherwise refused to sell government property).[9]

William also accepted a position as aide-de-camp to Governor Edward Coles of Illinois in 1825. As part of his duties and because of his father's relationship to the Revolutionary War hero, William had the opportunity to serve Marie-Joseph Paul Yves Roch Gilbert du Motier, Marquis de Lafayette.

Born in 1757, Lafayette was a French aristocrat who voluntarily joined George Washington's army and entered the American Revolutionary War to support the patriotic fight against the British for freedom and liberty. He used his own money to pay for his expenses, including his uniform. He served heroically at the Battle of Brandywine in 1777 and was present at Valley Forge and at Yorktown. Greatly admired by Washington and Hamilton, Lafayette became a lifelong friend to both.

After the announcement of the Monroe Doctrine, President James Monroe and the US Congress sent a formal invitation to General Lafayette asking him to revisit the country he had helped lead to independence. Lafayette accepted the invitation and sailed from France, arriving in New York in 1824. His visit rekindled patriotic sentiment throughout America.

In Illinois, William served on a joint state house and senate committee and helped to draft "an address inviting Lafayette to visit the state."[10] After traversing various towns on the East Coast, Lafayette traveled aboard the *Natchez* to Saint Louis, where he was received with great pomp and show. The founder of Saint Louis, Auguste Choteau, escorted him in a carriage drawn by four horses to the house of Choteau's son. There, Lafayette was welcomed by many visitors, including William.[11] Coles introduced William to Lafayette through a letter: "This will be handed to you by my friend and aid de camp Col: William Schuyler Hamilton, who I take a peculiar pleasure in introducing to you, as the son of your old and particular friend Gen: Alexander Hamilton."[12] Lafayette received William, "son of the General Alexander Hamilton . . . whom General Lafayette had loved so much," with the greatest "pleasure."[13] During Lafayette's visit, William, who spoke French eloquently, acted as his interpreter.[14] Lafayette remained in America for thirteen months before returning to France in September 1825.

To avoid any undue confusion, a note about William's middle name is due. William was born William Stephen Hamilton. At some point after his move to the Midwest, he seems to have changed his name to William Schuyler Hamilton. For this reason, Rector, Coles, and even his friend Stephenson addressed him as William Schuyler Hamilton instead of William Stephen Hamilton. So why did William change his name? It is possible that he wanted to give himself additional prestige and power, and the name Schuyler was as important, and perhaps even more so, than Hamilton in some circles. However, considering William's relocation to the frontier, there may be another reason for the change: he may have chosen to change his name in homage to his mother. Philip Hamilton wrote to Woodman indicating that William once rode his horse from the Midwest to New York just to visit his mother.[15]

That his mother loved him and worried about him is evident in her actions. In 1837, at the age of eighty, Elizabeth Hamilton, along with her daughter Eliza and son-in-law Sidney Holly, traveled to the Wisconsin Territory under the most trying circumstances, just to spend time with her beloved son. She wrote about her journey to her youngest son back in New York: "I have passed the Ohio, the river is very spacious, but very difficult to navigation, the shores beautiful and the vessel approaching the shore at the distance of one dozen feet; no warf, the water is so mixed with clay that it is not drinkable without wine. This evening we shall be at St. Louis on the Mississippi. Our passage will be tedious as we go against the stream."[16] During her stay with William, Elizabeth Hamilton stayed with the Gratiots and visited Lake Calhoun and the falls of Minnehaha and Saint Anthony. She also attended a military parade held in her honor at Fort Snelling.[17] Months later, she returned home to the East Coast without realizing that it was the last time she would ever see her son.

Elizabeth Hamilton survived her son by four years, but the news of William's death never reached her, and she "hungered after her son until she went to her grave." His death was kept a secret from her because the rest of her children worried about her health.[18] After he had left New York and relocated to the Midwest, William seldom had the opportunity to see his mother. He may have taken her name as his middle name for sentimental reasons. However, no evidence supports either explanation for the change; either possibility remains as good a guess as the other.

The Northwest Territory incorporated the area that is now the state of Wisconsin. After Ohio's admission into the Union as a state in 1803, Wisconsin dangled between the Indiana and Illinois Territories. That later changed when Indiana became a state in 1816 and Illinois followed in 1818, making Wisconsin part of the Michigan Territory. The end of the War of 1812 further opened the region to American settlers. By the 1820s the fur trade began to lose its power in the region, but a new, more profitable product made a move to the upper Illinois area promising: "gray gold," or lead. By 1827, people on the frontier were scrambling to secure land where they could find lead.

The upper Illinois and southwestern region of Wisconsin had heavy lead deposits. The Native Americans had been aware of the lead for years. Settlers began arriving in the early nineteenth century, and the influx of people searching for lead increased the population and development in Galena, which soon became a popular city in Illinois. From Galena, people often traveled farther north and into the southern part of Wisconsin in search of lead deposits.

Galena is a bluish-gray cubic mineral that has a metallic shine and is made of the purest lead. The city of Galena derived its name from the mineral, which was abundant in the region. Galena today is a quaint city rich in history situated along the scenic Galena River (Fever River) in the northern part of Illinois. Before the Civil War, President Ulysses S. Grant once resided in Galena. At a distance from Grant's house stands the beautiful Victorian house of William's friend and fellow politician Elihu B. Washburne. Downtown Galena boasts a development of beautiful red brick historical homes with nineteenth-century architectural details. The city is in the midst of hill country, with the Galena River running right through the center of town. The same river brought William and two of his friends, James D. Brents and Daniel M. Parkinson, to Galena in 1827 on the Fourth of July.[19]

When William arrived in the area, he learned of a Native American attack led by a Winnebago named Red Bird and his warriors. The Red Bird Disturbance of 1827, also known as the Winnebago War, was a brief attack of the Winnebago on the white settlers. The Winnebago, thinking that two of their warriors had been killed by the US Army, decided to avenge their deaths. The first attack took place in the white settlement at Prairie du Chien, where Red Bird and his companions killed two men and severely injured a baby. Later, the Winnebago warriors attacked a group of white men who were returning from carrying supplies to Fort Snelling in a keelboat. The warriors killed two of the men and injured four more. Much to the dismay of Governor Lewis Cass of the Michigan Territory, the news of the attack spread quickly throughout the region, causing panic within the settler community. Soon, the local militia units organized at Prairie du Chien to answer Cass's urgent call for help. William volunteered to serve under the leadership of Captain Abner Fields of Vandalia, Illinois.[20] The volunteers assembled at Prairie du Chien to help defend the area until military support could arrive. William's role in the skirmish was minor, but it was his first chance to use his West Point military training. He also had the opportunity to help with peaceful negotiations between the Winnebago and the settlers.[21] In the end, Red Bird surrendered and signed a peace treaty with the United States, thereby concluding the Winnebago War. He was imprisoned and died in jail a year later.

After the Winnebago War, William mined in Galena for some time, then ventured farther north in search of greater lead deposits, arriving in the area that is now Wiota, Wisconsin.

NOTES

1. William Stephen Hamilton to E. D. Taylor, promissory note, August 10, 1825, Abraham Lincoln Presidential Library.

2. William Stephen Hamilton to John C. Hamilton, August 6, 1819, Hamilton Family MSS.

3. *History of Sangamon County*, 280.

4. Ford, *History of Illinois*, 58.

5. "Alexander Hamilton's Son Surveyed Peoria," 1.

6. Dixon, *First Plat of Peoria*, 1826.

7. Ingersoll, *History of Peoria County*, 334.

8. Moon, "Story of Nom-A-Que," 246–255.

9. Smith, "Personal Narrative of William S. Hamilton," 339–342.

10. Greene and Alvord, *Governor's Letter Books*, 70.

11. Levasseur, *Lafayette in America*, 394.

12. Washburne, *Sketch of Edward Coles*, 189–190.

13. Levasseur, *Lafayette in America*, 394.

14. Rennick, "Peoria and Galena Trail," 419.

15. Philip Hamilton to Cyrus Woodman, February 7, 1880, Woodman MSS.

16. Allan McLane Hamilton, *Intimate Life of Alexander Hamilton*, 221.

17. Gratiot, "Mrs. Gratiot's Narrative," 274–275.

18. Edgar A. Hamilton to Cyrus Woodman, January 23, 1880, Woodman MSS.

19. Daniel M. Parkinson, *Pioneer Life in Wisconsin*, 329.

20. Daniel M. Parkinson, 330.

21. Muldoon, *Alexander Hamilton's Pioneer Son*, 56.

FOUR

Black Hawk War

ALTHOUGH THE BLACK HAWK WAR OCCURRED IN 1832, THE
seeds of the confrontation began much earlier. Prior to the nineteenth
century, the United States had signed various treaties with the eastern
Native American tribes requiring them to surrender their land. But
these treaties did not resolve the growing conflict between Native
Americans and settlers moving westward. In 1804, Governor William
Henry Harrison of the Indiana Territory had signed a treaty with
representatives of the Sauk and Fox tribes that gave them an annuity
of $1,000 for fifty million acres of land between the Wisconsin River,
the Fox of Illinois, the Illinois, the Mississippi, and the eastern part
of Missouri.[1] As the century progressed, the desire for western lands
continued to increase the flow of settlers into the frontier.

Harrison came from an aristocratic Virginia planter family. Born
in 1773, he attended Hampden-Sydney College. In 1791, he accepted a
commission as ensign in the First Infantry of the Regular Army and
served as aide-de-camp to General "Mad Anthony" Wayne during
the Battle of Fallen Timbers. He became secretary of the Northwest
Territory in 1798 and then governor of the Indiana Territory in 1801,
a position he held for the next twelve years.

By 1811, two Shawnee brothers in the Northwest, Chief Tecumseh and Tenskwatawa, also known as the Prophet, formed a strong

confederation against the United States. Born in 1768 to a Shawnee war
chief named Puckshinwau and a Shawnee mother named Methotaske,
Tecumseh came of age during the French and Indian War. After the
death of his father at the Battle of Point Pleasant during Lord Dun-
more's War, Tecumseh decided to become a warrior too. He joined the
American Indian Confederacy under the Mohawk chief Joseph Bry-
ant. He fought and defeated General Arthur St. Clair and his army at
the Battle of Wabash. In 1794, Tecumseh was also present at the Battle
of Fallen Timbers, where he was defeated by General Wayne.

After the defeat at Fallen Timbers, Tecumseh joined his brother
Tenskwatawa at Prophetstown, Indiana Territory, and they formed
an alliance to fight against the encroaching settlers and the American
government. In 1809, Harrison signed the Treaty of Fort Wayne. The
treaty required Indiana Native American tribes to sell three million
acres of land to the US government. It further energized Tecumseh to
build his army. To this purpose, he traveled to Canada and Alabama
to recruit men.

On the evening of November 6, 1811, Tecumseh was out recruiting
men for his cause when Harrison led almost a thousand militiamen
and soldiers to Tecumseh's village at Prophetstown. When he arrived,
he was met with a white flag of truce carried by a warrior sent by
Tenskwatawa. Before leaving Prophetstown, Tecumseh had warned
Tenskwatawa not to engage in any act of war. Thus, Tenskwatawa
asked Harrison for some time to have a peaceful discussion. Harrison
agreed to his request and ordered his men to set up camp for the night
near Burnett Creek, almost a mile away from Prophetstown.

As the army under Harrison rested, Tenskwatawa stood above a
rock (now called Prophet's Rock) and challenged his warriors to fight
against the Americans. Chanting battle songs and promising that they
would be protected from bullets, Tenskwatawa ignored his brother's
warning and led his warriors to attack Harrison and his army.

By dawn on November 7, 1811, Harrison found himself and his men
surrounded by Tenskwatawa's warriors. The warriors fired the first
shots at Harrison and his troops at the Battle of Tippecanoe. Harrison ordered his men under the Indiana Mounted Rifles to defend

the southern section that the warriors had broken through. At first it worked, and the warriors withdrew. But they soon turned and attacked Harrison and his men again, focusing on the southern section. The Battle of Tippecanoe lasted for two hours, but Harrison's army was too great an enemy for Tenskwatawa and his warriors. Beaten back, the warriors returned to Prophetstown and turned on Tenskwatawa. They eventually abandoned Prophetstown. Without Tecumseh, there was no way to stop them from leaving the village.

The following day, Harrison burned Prophetstown to the ground and marched back to Vincennes. When Tecumseh returned three months later, he found Prophetstown in a complete ruin. But more than his village was destroyed. The defeat of Tecumseh's men at the Battle of Tippecanoe also ended his vision for a strong Native American confederacy.

Yet even after their defeat, several Native American tribes in the Great Lakes region worked alongside the British to fight the United States in the War of 1812. By the 1820s, the United States favored removal of the Native Americans from the Ohio Valley to Georgia. Those tribes that remained felt increased pressure from incoming settlers. Then, in May 1830, Congress passed the Indian Removal Act, which would have dire consequences for the Native American population.

By the early 1830s, Black Hawk, also known as Ma-ka-tai-me-she-kia-kiak, a war chief and leader of the Sauk nation, challenged the legitimacy of the 1804 treaty that had been signed with the United States. Black Hawk was born in 1767 in Saukenuk, Illinois. He aligned himself with the British during the War of 1812 and fought against the US Army in an effort to stop further encroachment into the Sauk land. Black Hawk's "British Band" was named thus because it held the severest anti-American sentiment and included warriors from the Sauks, the Meskwakis, and the Kickapoos. Black Hawk argued that the 1804 treaty was signed by people who were unauthorized to speak on behalf of his nation. The federal government disagreed.

Black Hawk's rival was a war chief named Ke-o-kuk, who was a member of the Fox tribe and who later became a leading member of the Sauk assembly. Although Ke-o-kuk distrusted Americans too, he agreed to deal diplomatically with the United States because he had witnessed the might of the nation on a trip to Washington, DC, in 1824. Therefore, he was more obliged than Black Hawk to honor the 1804 treaty. On July 15, 1830, he signed a treaty ceding over twenty-six million acres of Sauk land. Black Hawk did not agree with the treaty, and he refused to give up the land that had belonged to his ancestors. He tried to appeal to the government to disregard the treaty.

However, President Jackson's administration forced all Native American tribes east of the Mississippi, including the nation to which Black Hawk belonged, to leave their ancestral homelands. The harsh winter of 1832 made the prospect of moving farther from their land even more unappealing to Black Hawk. After several futile attempts to resolve the matter with the US government, Black Hawk led almost two thousand people of the Sauk and Fox nations back to the area that they had lost. In the spring of 1832, Black Hawk crossed the Mississippi River and entered Illinois.

News of Black Hawk's movements spread fast. Illinois Governor John Reynolds put out a call for volunteers to assemble as his army to combat Black Hawk and his warriors. At the time, US troops were stationed under the command of General Henry Atkinson at Jefferson Barracks in Saint Louis, Missouri. Born in 1782 in Person County, North Carolina, Atkinson joined the US Army at the age of twenty-six. He served as a colonel in the War of 1812. Afterward, he negotiated peace treaties with the Native American tribes of the Upper Missouri. Atkinson was a good administrator, less so a military commander. But by 1832, he was in full command of those of the US military who participated in the Black Hawk War.

At the outset of the war, Atkinson led his men from Jefferson Barracks to Fort Armstrong on Rock Island. From that point, they used keelboats to make their way to Dixon's Ferry, which became "the general rendezvous of all the troops coming in."[2] Atkinson sent two messages to Black Hawk ordering him to fall back, but Black Hawk refused to comply.[3] Instead, by April 25, Black Hawk and his British Band were moving on the eastern side of Rock River.

Meanwhile, Major Isaiah Stillman, a merchant from Canton in charge of 275 Illinois militiamen, had been waiting at Dixon's Ferry "with abundance of ammunitions and supplies" for Atkinson to arrive. His men were "impatient at the slow advance of the army and anxious at once to do something brilliant." So they demanded to be allowed to go after Black Hawk without waiting for the regulars to arrive.[4] Reynolds granted them permission to proceed, and they headed out on May 12, camping near White Rock Grove later that night.[5]

According to Black Hawk, the next day, when he heard that a troop of "three or four hundred white men, on horse-back" were seen in the area, he sent three of his warriors under the banner of a white flag to meet the Americans "and conduct them to our camp, that we might hold a council with them." He was even willing to "go and see them" on his own if necessary. He then sent five other warriors to follow the first party "to see what might take place." But the Americans' inability to understand the Native American language led to miscommunication and an unexpected result. Instead of negotiating peacefully, the Americans captured warriors from Black Hawk's first party and chased and killed some from the second party. Two of them managed to escape and returned to Black Hawk with the news. Angered by the treatment of his men, Black Hawk "raised a yell" and called his warriors to fight back. He had been "forced into war." As the day drew to a close, the British Band charged toward the Americans with a vengeance and attacked them in the open prairie with just "a few bushes between [them]." To Black Hawk's consternation, Stillman's troop retreated "without showing fight."[6] The militiamen could not maintain order, and they scattered in every direction, leaving Black Hawk and his British Band victorious in this first major battle of the Black Hawk War, called Stillman's Run.

Aside from Black Hawk's victory, Stillman's Run is also famous as the battle site Lincoln mentioned years later when he discussed his service in the Black Hawk War. Although no evidence indicates that Lincoln and William knew each other, it is plausible that they may have met at some point. In many ways, before he left Illinois and became president of the United States, Lincoln had followed a path similar to William's. Both were from Sangamon County, and they may have known many of the same people. Both had worked as surveyors and lawyers, and they were elected legislators from the same county at different times. Both also served in the Black Hawk War and were in the same vicinity on more than one occasion.

On May 15, US troops, including Lincoln and his company, which was under the command of General Whiteside, marched to the site of Stillman's Run. They arrived late in the evening and found "bodies scalped and mangled." That night they set camp near the battlefield. The next morning, Lincoln and the other soldiers buried the dead before marching back to Dixon's Ferry. On May 17, Lincoln and his company drew "10 quarts of meal and 10 pounds of pork." On May 18, William was dispatched with his spies to the battlefield. These dates show that both men were at Dixon's Ferry in the same month and quite possibly on the same days. But the dates that confirm that both men were on the same spot are May 21 and June 13.

On May 21 "the Army met William S. Hamilton at noon about six miles below Kishwaukee River," and the "volunteers apparently follow trail which is sometimes distant from river, but they encamp on river each night with regulars who are in charge of keelboats." Lincoln was mustered out of the US Army on May 27, and "he then enrolls in company of Capt. Elijah Iles for service in 20-day regiment." The same Captain Iles marched his company to Dixon's Ferry on June 13 as "they pass camp of 170 Sioux, Menominee, and Winnebago Indians under command of Col. William S. Hamilton."[7] William, under the instructions of General Atkinson, had set off "to go and bring on the Menominees and Sioux Indians to the number of 1000 or under."[8] Again, Dixon's Ferry was the common base for all military and militia troops during the Black Hawk War. These dates show at least two incidents when William and Lincoln could have been together.

The news of Stillman's defeat and of subsequent attacks on settlers spread fast throughout the region. Town meetings were called to decide how to prepare for war. In Galena, the citizens asked "that an enrolment of all persons subject to military duty, be immediately made, and held in readiness for active service; and to parade with their arms and equipment every evening at 4 o'clock."[9] At Hamilton's Diggings, William engaged his men to help him build a fort to protect the miners and their families. William and his men built Fort Hamilton within a month, constructing a "large stockade of sharp-pointed logs, with two block houses on corners diagonally opposite" each other. The entire fort "was forty feet square, surrounded by a ditch and pickets."[10] Noticing a shortage of weapons, the ever-resourceful William equipped his miners with guns and with ammunition he constructed using wood, horseshoe iron, and molten lead.[11] Then, placing his friend Captain George W. Harrison in charge of the fort, William left for Dixon's Ferry.[12]

William volunteered to work as a scout for the militia of Iowa County, Michigan Territory, under the command of Colonel Henry Dodge. Dodge had also participated previously in the Winnebago War. On May 2, William joined Dodge's ranks as the captain of the first mounted company.[13] William left Dixon for Fort Crawford at Prairie du Chien sometime on May 26, to find the Menominees and the Santee Sioux, who were enemies of the Sauk and Fox tribes. He hazarded the possible attacks of Black Hawk's British Band and the hidden dangers of nature and managed to find his way to Fort Crawford. On his arrival, William handed the Indian agent, General Joseph Street, a letter from General Atkinson requesting "you send me at this place, with as little delay as possible, as many Menomonee and Sioux Indians as can be collected within striking distance of Prairie du Chien." Atkinson needed to "employ them in conjunction with the troops against the Sauks and the Foxes, who are now some fifty miles above [them] in a state of war against the whites." But there were no such Indians to be found right away, so Street ordered one of his men, J. P. Burnett, "to use every means to expedite the object" and to bring back any Menominees and Sioux who wanted to travel to Dixon's Ferry with William. Within six days, Street received communication from Burnett that he had located a group of Santee Sioux and Winnebagos who "appear well affected towards the whites, are in fine spirits, and seem anxious to engage with the Sauks and Foxes."[14]

Ready and willing as they were to fight with their archenemies, the Winnebagos, Santee Sioux, and Menominee warriors were less interested in following the rules of war set by the US military. They followed William to Fort Hamilton and stayed long enough to eat "up a great deal of [their] beef" before becoming "discontented" and leaving, "frightening the inhabitants of the country through which they passed" in the process.[15]

Six warriors remained with William, but those who returned to Prairie du Chien complained about William to Street. When he asked them why they had returned without fighting against their enemies, they replied, "You sent us with a little man," and "We followed him a great way over large wagon roads that were very hard and our moccasins are worn out, and our feet sore; we can walk no further." Despite the rough travel, the warriors had not seen any large army at Fort Hamilton, and they felt that William "did not use [them] well, and [they] turned and came back to [Street]." But Street found no basis for their complaints. Some of General Dodge's men who were then visiting from Fort Hamilton had already informed him that back at Fort Hamilton the warriors "were kindly treated, and provisions were plenty, and were issued to [them] freely." Furthermore, Street was told that the warriors had left Fort Hamilton under false pretenses, telling Dodge's men that they were leaving "to get new moccasins, and would return in a few days."[16] Catching them in a lie, Street decided to dismiss them, and they went back home.

On June 14, a band of Black Hawk's warriors headed toward Fort Hamilton. Six miles from the fort, they discovered some men working in a cornfield. The farm belonged to a man named Omri Spafford, who, along with his five companions, Abraham Searles, Bennett Million, Frances Spencer, James McIlwaine, and John Bull, was working in the field. The warriors attacked the men, and chaos ensued as the men tried to dodge their assailants to no avail. The warring party killed Spafford on the spot. Spencer ran and hid "under the floor of an old or hog-pen," and a few days later the settlers found him "nearly crazed with fright." The other men jumped in the river and tried to swim to the other bank, but the warriors shot and killed them.[17]

Somehow, despite being pursued by the warriors, Million survived and found his way back to the fort.

On hearing the news of Spafford's farm, Colonel Henry Dodge sent a dozen men to Fort Hamilton under the command of Major R. H. Kirkpatrick. The men arrived late at night on June 15. The next day, they located and buried the bodies of the farmer and his companions. Later in the day, Dodge arrived at Fort Hamilton with more of his men. Even before he had an opportunity to restore order, "the firing of gun shots was heard" from a distance. Dodge immediately took a party of twenty-one men, including some of William's miners, and gave chase to Black Hawk's warring party. They traveled through swampy water and heavy undergrowth until they found the warriors. Both sides fired shots, and then the men appeared "face to face" against one another, ready for hand-to-hand combat. The Battle of Pecatonica (also known as the Battle of Horseshoe Bend) ensued, and Dodge's men triumphed.[18]

William arrived at Fort Hamilton with his band of warriors within an hour after the Battle of Pecatonica ended.[19] He remained in charge of his team, which made up the scouting party under Dodge's command. A few days later, a Winnebago chief named White Crow arrived at the camp and agreed to help Dodge's men find Black Hawk's hideout. For days he led the men toward Rock River, where Black Hawk was supposed to be camping. But William and his men discovered that Black Hawk had "decamped" from the area and held "a most advantageous position for defense." Dodge's men agreed that White Crow was "acting in concert with Black Hawk" and that had it not been for the discovery made by William and his scouts, "the volunteers must, if not beaten, at least, have suffered severely."[20]

For his "valor and patriotism," the "Ladies of the Lead Mines" presented William with a US flag. He accepted the honor and found it "highly gratifying." He vowed "that [his] utmost exertion shall be used to relieve, with aft possible speed, our unhappy country, and bring the war to such an issue as will insure lasting peace."[21] But finding the enemy was a secondary matter; finding enough help to search for the British Band was becoming problematic.

By July, General Atkinson needed to replenish his depleting army. He again sent William scouting, this time with a message to Colonel George Boyd, the Indian agent in Green Bay.[22] Atkinson requested the immediate enlistment of any Menominees willing to fight for the Americans, to be sent back to him under William's command. Although Boyd procured the assistance of two hundred Menominees for the service, he could not convince them to follow William because they "demanded as a favor, that in the event Menominees being called into the field, that Colo. Samuel C. Stambaugh should be placed at their head." Stambaugh was the former Indian agent to the Menominee people. Understandably, they favored him over William. Yet Boyd's "earnest wish was to employ the talents and experience of Colo. Hamilton, by associating him with the expedition, with that rank which would bring him second in command." But William "at once declined" to accept the offer.[23] Perhaps William was not interested in playing second fiddle to Stambaugh, or maybe he preferred working alone instead of trying to implement discipline for a group of Native American warriors who had their own ways of fighting in battles, as William had already experienced.

Through his scouting to find Black Hawk, William discovered that Black Hawk and his warriors were traveling near the Wisconsin River. He shared the information with Stambaugh, who set out with his troop, which included a group of Menominee warriors, to capture them. On arriving near Cassville, Stambaugh and his men discovered "the smoke of the Indians encamped in a low spot beside a stream in the prairie." Stambaugh's men were directed to capture the two men, few women, and children, "but the Menominee were fierce for a fight, and killed the two men, and took the other prisoners." There are conflicting accounts of William's presence and participation in the event. In his memoirs, Augustin Grignon, who served in the conflict, stated that "Col. Hamilton participated in it."[24] But William Powell, also present at the scene, stated that "Augustin Grignon is mistaken in saying that Col. William S. Hamilton had anything to do with this expedition, for he had not, and was not along."[25] If William was present, it is difficult to imagine him participating in the slaughter, considering his disposition toward women in general and his previous attempts to maintain order with the Menominees. His rejection of Boyd's proposal to be second in command to Stambaugh over the Menominees—a Native American nation that had already shown disdain for William's authority—also makes it questionable whether he approved of such methods of warfare.

Black Hawk tried to escape with his people, including warriors, women, and children, by making his way to the Mississippi River. But they were exhausted, starving, and low on morale. As Black Hawk tried to plan his next move, the privately owned steamboat *Warrior*, put into service for the US government, appeared. Black Hawk tried to surrender, but the *Warrior*, not trusting him, fired at his people. Twenty-five warriors were killed, but Black Hawk managed to escape with some of his people, and they went into hiding near Tomah, Wisconsin. The following morning, the US military found the remaining Sauks who were attempting to cross the river and fired at them. The *Warrior* joined them again, firing cannons at anyone trying to swim across the river. Those Sauks who did manage to cross over were killed by their enemies, the Santee Sioux, who were waiting for them on the opposite bank. The gruesome incident became known as the Massacre at Bad Axe, and it ended the Black Hawk War.

By the conclusion of the Black Hawk War, William had served as a volunteer scout for the army for three months. The war had brought men from the region together to fight against a common enemy. But it had also brought out challenges within the ranks. Deadly disease, hunger, sheer exhaustion, pride, arrogance, and petty differences often developed when men clustered together for a long period of time. William had experienced his own share of squabbles with the men he had led and with those he had followed in the Black Hawk War.

The end of the Black Hawk War opened up the land that had once been home to various Native American tribes for exploration by the settlers. More of them arrived and helped settle the upper part of the Great Lakes region. New towns formed and began to flourish. With the war behind him, William once again turned his attention to his home, Wiota.

NOTES

1. Black Hawk, *Life of Black Hawk*, xii.
2. Anderson, "Reminiscences of the Black Hawk War," 169.
3. Draper, "Story of the Black Hawk War," 233.
4. Draper, 235.
5. Chapman, *History of Fulton County Illinois*, 292.
6. Black Hawk, *Life of Black Hawk*, 58, 60–61.
7. Baringer, *Lincoln Day by Day*, 21–23, 25.
8. "Seat of War," June 6, 1832.
9. "Seat of War," June 6, 1832.
10. Conley, "Early History of Lafayette County," 324.
11. DeForest, "Primitive Gunnery," 3.
12. Muldoon, *Alexander Hamilton's Pioneer Son*, 93. In his biography of William, Muldoon states that Captain Harrison was the son of President William Henry Harrison. Captain Harrison may have been related to William Henry Harrison, but he was not the son of the ninth president of the United States.
13. Salter, *Life of Henry Dodge*, 45.
14. Burnett, "Memoir of Thomas Pendleton Burnett," 256–257.
15. Daniel M. Parkinson, "Pioneer Life in Wisconsin," 350.
16. Street, "Sioux and the Black Hawk War," 314.
17. Salisbury, "Green County Pioneers," 404.
18. Peter Parkinson Jr., "Notes on the Black Hawk War," 193–196.
19. Strong, "Indian Wars of Wisconsin," 278.
20. Daniel M. Parkinson, "Pioneer Life in Wisconsin," 354.
21. *Galenian*, July 4, 1832.
22. Whitney, *Black Hawk War*, 563.
23. Tanner, "Papers of Indian Agent Boyd, 1832," 272.
24. Grignon, "Seventy-Two Years' Recollections of Wisconsin," 295.
25. Powell, "William Powell's Recollections," 166.

William Stephen Hamilton portrait photo. Wisconsin Historical Society, WHS-3458.

Alexander Hamilton portrait painting. © A. K. Fielding/Trehan's Treasures Studio.

Elizabeth Hamilton portrait drawing. © A. K. Fielding/Trehan's Treasures
Studio.

Cyrus Woodman portrait drawing. © A. K. Fielding/Trehan's Treasures
Studio.

FIVE

Gray Gold

THE BEAUTY AND MAJESTY OF THE BLUE MOUND IN Wisconsin can be seen from miles away. In late summer, the cool breeze sways the green grass and golden cornstalks covering acres of land. It rustles the leaves of the region's popular walnut trees, mimicking the soothing sound of ocean waves. Eagles fly high above in a crystal-blue sky as the cows and horses graze in the valley below, evoking a time when pioneers cleared the land and settled the area. Today, a forty-five-minute drive on Highway 78 from Galena, Illinois, through the beautiful valleys of Wisconsin leads straight to the place that William called home.

Highway 78 cuts through the center of Mineral Point, once a booming lead-mining town that now stands divided by a four-way stop sign. A few buildings from the nineteenth century still exist, surrounded by quaint antique shops and eateries. In William's time, Mineral Point formed the center of activity in the lead region. It thrived with businesses that brought all sorts of people from surrounding areas, including miners, gamblers, drinkers, fugitives, drovers, deserters, thieves, prostitutes, and vagabonds. Gambling, quarreling, fighting, and even dueling were not uncommon in such a male-dominated society. Like other miners in the region, William frequented the area and mixed with interesting characters.

William's presence in the region may explain Rodolf's assessment
of him as a gambler. The frontier was a harsh place because of the
natural elements and the economic, social, and political conditions
of the time. Only the toughest could survive. Quarrelsome companions, lack of money or food, or the possible threat of a Native
American attack—real or imagined—forced most pioneers to either
cower in fear or become fearless, brash, and brutal. Still others, such
as William, were able to maintain a level of decency that they had
acquired in the older states. William preferred to tackle the brutal
harshness of the Midwest, but he managed to preserve his dignified
upbringing when the occasion demanded.

Beyond Mineral Point, in the southern region of Wisconsin, is the
town of Wiota, founded by William and once known as Hamilton's
Diggings. Wiota is a much smaller town than Mineral Point, easy
to miss altogether on the one-lane highway. Situated in Lafayette
County, Wiota remains unincorporated, with less than a thousand
residents. A few nineteenth-century houses remain, but most of what
existed in William's day is long gone.

William himself dismantled and destroyed Fort Hamilton after
the Black Hawk War. Over the years, the locals erected a large sign
with a painted picture of what Fort Hamilton may have looked like
in the nineteenth century. The sign gives some information about
the fort, but its position alongside the main road makes it difficult
for visitors to read about the historical significance of the area. The
paint has deteriorated as time and the elements have attacked the surface, making it even harder to see it from a distance. The sign stands
within a small garden, with two small shrubs planted on either side.
Two American flags stand in front of the sign. The park itself is small
and enclosed by a rusty, dented metal rail that marks the road. There
are two stone markers within the park, one of which is dedicated to
a World War II soldier.

Behind the sign stands the Zimmerman Cheese Factory, and on the
other end is a road sign marked, ironically enough, "Dead Zone." A
large, noisy machine, belonging to the Zimmerman Cheese Factory,
hovers over the sign, making the park seem more like an eyesore than

a place for people to visit and contemplate the past. An absence of historic markers and parking area make it difficult for visitors to enter the place. The locals believe that most people only stop by the sign if they are visiting the Zimmerman Cheese Factory.

Nineteenth-century Wiota was quite different. William's contemporary and friend Moses Strong, who was a land agent in the lead region of Wisconsin, once described Hamilton's Diggings as an "extensive and very valuable lead diggings," an area thriving with "three taverns, two or three stores, two or three blacksmith shops," among other things.[1] It was remarkable for a town in this section of the Midwest to experience such growth during the early nineteenth century.

The actual site of Fort Hamilton is a farmland now owned by a private party. Getting to the spot where Fort Hamilton once stood requires a drive or walk across private farmland, followed by a climb over a barbed-wire fence. The area no longer resembles a fort; the sole "markers" indicating where the fort once stood are the indentations in the earth itself that have lasted over 180 years. The grass is thick and lush, and the wide-open area allows for a wonderful view. A few paces away, a small creek gurgles. William and his men once smelted lead in the same spot. Most of the creek is now dry, with grass, dead trees, and rocks forming the only signs left from William's days. Among the many rocks near the creek, I discovered one in 2012, during my research for this book, that contained bits of lead deposits that may have come from William's operation.

When the federal government began leasing parcels of land to miners, William placed his request for one and began his search for lead deposits in the region. By 1827, he had started his lead-mining business in the area that would become Hamilton's Diggings. Henceforth, and until his departure for California, he remained in the Midwest except when he traveled on business or to New York on horseback to visit his mother.[2] When he arrived, the prairie land was full of wildlife, including wolves, rattlesnakes, deer, prairie chickens, ducks, geese, and quail. Oak, maple, apple, and walnut trees were scattered throughout the valley in abundance. Considering William's appreciation of nature from early in his life, he must have loved the sight.

Indeed, it was not uncommon for William to go on long treks across the region even in the midst of a cold winter day just to visit a friend.[3]

Most miners, however, were more interested in digging for lead than enjoying the natural beauty of the area.[4] They dug ditches in the ground in their search for lead. Sometimes they used the holes as a temporary shack to sleep in when they were working in the fields. It is from these makeshift homes, called "badger holes," that Wisconsin gets its nickname: the Badger State. Some of them remain noticeable today, serving as a reminder of another time in our nation's history.

On his visit to the region, Rodolf saw the holes and "scores of men digging and prospecting for mineral, and windlasses in operation." He described the homestead of the Gratiots, William's friends, in vivid detail:

> Gratiot's Grove presented even at this early season a most charming prospect; as it appeared a month later. I have never seen it surpassed in Wisconsin. Before us lay a rolling prairie, bounded on the north by Blue Mound about thirty miles distant, and extending east to the Peckatonica River, whose course could be traced faintly by wooded hills; the prairie was bounded on the south and west by a magnificent grove of oaks, the destruction of which had been, however, already begun, as the voracious smelting furnaces mercilessly claimed the sacrifice of the splendid trees which were the pride and glory of the "Grove."[5]

As the price of lead climbed between 1827 and 1829, a plethora of miners arrived in the new territory. Men from Illinois, Indiana, Missouri, Virginia, New York, and North Carolina were among the first miners to arrive in the lead region. These were followed by men from other lands, such as England, Ireland, Wales, Canada, and Scotland. Many of these miners made their way to Hamilton's Diggings.

Although some miners used tents or lived in their wagons until they could build houses for themselves, self-reliant and innovative William began to build his house in the vicinity of his lead mine. He cleared the land and prepared it to build the structure for what would become his home for much of his adult life. Building materials were limited, and so was the help necessary to build great and fancy homes. From contemporary accounts it is known that William had a "house" and probably "felled trees, cut the trunks to the required length, smoothed them on two sides," and used them to build the walls. He also used "clapboards split by hand" to form the roof of the house. The house also had a fireplace. Many such fireplaces in pioneer homes were made "sometimes of stone" but "usually of mud."[6] He used some of the logs to carve out chairs and a table for his home. Crude as it may have looked, the furniture and the cabin well served his purpose on the frontier.

Kinzie's description of William's home creates a vivid picture. She noted in detail that the house had a fireplace and that "a large fire was burning in the clay chimney, and the room was of a genial warmth, notwithstanding the apertures, many inches in width, beside the doors and windows." The meal was "a plain, comfortable dinner" served on "a table as long as the dimensions of the cabin would admit" with one end "covered with somewhat nicer furniture and more delicate fare than the remaining portion."[7]

Others, such as Rodolf, were less kind in their assessment of William's humble home: "Although I did not expect to find a solid, strong, imposing structure, such as I had seen on the Rhine, nor a residence such as a colonel commanding a fort might be expected to occupy, yet I confess I had all romance taken out of me when I found the fort consisted of two small log cabins, connected with each other by an open area, covered by clapboards." Rodolf noted further details: "The doors had no bolts or locks but simply a latch-string hanging out; the single opening in each cabin, intended for a window, had, if I remember rightly, no glass." Unlike Kinzie, Rodolf felt that "the furniture corresponded with the building: a rude bedstead with some blankets and buffalo robes for bedding, an oaken table, some wooden stools." For him at least, "Hamilton's Diggings presented not nearly as handsome or pleasing a prospect as Gratiot's Grove. The hills were nearly bare of trees, having been cut down to feed the furnace; and although the mound at Belmont, the Platte Mound, and the Blue Mound formed the frame of the panorama, yet the view was not so extended and charming as from the Gratiot's." He did note, however, that "the prairie was cut up by numerous mineral holes, piles of dirt, and windlasses, which marred the beauty of the landscape, but showed great activity and industry."[8]

Whatever impression his home created on others, William built it as a perfect haven for his free spirit. His home was a welcome reprieve to his friends and even open to Native Americans. Edgar Hamilton told Woodman in a letter: "The Indians had a wholesome dread of him, but yet would do him many kindnesses . . . In the living room of uncle's cabin the Indians frequently gathered."[9] At any given time, William may have entertained his friends the Gratiots and the Kinzies, his hardworking miners, or even Native Americans.

Life on the frontier was grueling, but William was a man who shunned idleness. Lead mining was tough business, but far from being an overlord, William worked hard alongside his men. His miners admired him and began calling him the "Rough Diamond" because although his outward appearance was rough, to them, he was a true gem inside.[10]

In the eighteenth century, lead was imported from Great Britain, but by the nineteenth century, America was looking within to fill this need. Lead was used to make paint, which was then used on houses, ships, and bridges. There was also a demand for lead to produce common goods such as pipes and bullets. Lead was rarely found in its purest form. The mineral had to be dug out and then smelted in a furnace to be usable. Before the miners arrived, the Native Americans had used picks and shovels to remove the mineral from the surface. The miners used a different method to retrieve the lead buried deeper under the surface. They placed a shaft deep in the ground through a hole five feet wide. Once the area was secure, two men cranked a windlass to lower miners dangling from a rope into the ground. To dig for lead, the miners used simple tools such as a wooden bucket, a shovel, a pick, blasting powder, and a candle set in fire clay that stuck to the surface of the rock. They wore heavy shoes, overalls, and thick jackets made of bed ticking when working in the mines.

Once the lead was dug out, it had to be smelted. The smelting process required placing the mineral in a furnace built of limestone. The furnace had three walls, each measuring eight feet long by four feet wide and two feet thick. On both sides of the hearth was a shelf that measured a foot high and a foot wide. Large oak logs were placed on the shelf to create a makeshift bed for the mineral. The furnace was then packed with the mineral. Other logs were placed on top to cover it, and then the fire was lit. A hole, or "eye," opened at the lower end of an arched wall. A metal tub stood beneath the eye to catch the melted lead. The hot lead was carried from the tub in an iron dipper and poured into the pig lead molds, the casts used to make bars of lead. It took twenty-four hours to melt the lead. And it took just forty-eight hours of use for the furnace to crumble to nothingness.[11]

Not all miners were smelters. Not all smelters were miners. The government offered miners an opportunity to purchase a license to run a smelting operation, which allowed the use of timber and stone on the leased land. In return, the miner had to put up a $10,000 bond for the license and give one-tenth of all lead produced to the government as payment.[12] Those miners who did not have their own smelting operation sent the mineral fifty-five miles away to Galena in wagons to be smelted. Once the mineral was smelted, boats carried the load of lead to Saint Louis or New Orleans to market. The smelting process was lengthy and expensive. Suffice it to say that the smelting business was just possible for the wealthier miners.

William had discovered the largest mass of pure lead in the area, which had contributed to making him a wealthy miner.[13] That wealth allowed him to pay the bond money and construct a smelting operation at Hamilton's Diggings and to avoid the unnecessary expense and hassle of transporting the lead to Galena. Hamilton's Diggings was also strategically located near the Pecatonica River, which allowed William to send his ore on his flatboats to St. Louis for sale.[14] He was getting on better financially at this stage of his life than when he had first arrived in Saint Louis.

Hamilton's Diggings grew into a settlement as more miners and their families arrived in droves. With the population increase, William decided to name his town and called it Wiota, which means "joining of the waters."[15] He allowed Reverend Aaron Hawley to perform the earliest religious service.[16] In 1832, he opened a general store on the south side of the village to offer products and services to the miners and their families. One of the earliest US post offices in the Michigan Territory was located in William's grocery store, and he served as postmaster.[17] By 1838, another general store opened up to meet increasing demands.[18] The general stores provided much-needed items, such as hardware, cooking utensils, food, paints, medicine, books, and shoes. Furthermore, it provided the settlers with a venue to trade their goods, such as butter, eggs, cheese, meat, coffee, tea, and utensils. It also gave them an opportunity to receive mail and to catch up on the latest news and gossip. The first school opened on the east side of the village in 1833. Such a school would have provided children with an opportunity to learn how to spell, debate, and sing.[19] These early schools were one-story log houses that often doubled as courtrooms or churches.[20] During the organization of the Territory of Wisconsin in 1836, the legislative body approved the plan for a university and banking institutions. William became a trustee of the University of Madison and a stockholder of the Mineral Point bank.[21] By 1837, William had also founded another settlement, named Muscoda (also called English Prairie), by building another smelting furnace near the Wisconsin River.[22] A record of the year 1839 shows William's brother-in-law and Eliza's husband, Sidney A. Holly, listed as the postmaster of Muscoda. He was paid $5.68 for his position.[23] But within a few years, Holly was back in New York and then dead by 1842. Meanwhile, back in Wiota, a sawmill, a gristmill, and a log distillery soon all stood within a four-mile radius of the town.[24]

As important as Wiota had once been, it began to lose its significance as the century progressed. By 1847, it cost more to run the mine than the net profit the miners received from the sale of lead. William himself left Wiota, in part because running his mines had become expensive and he needed more money to continue the operation. Modern cost-effective methods of mining using new technology were introduced in the latter half of the nineteenth century. These methods, however, were used for zinc.[25] The decline of lead-mining towns such as Wiota was an unfortunate but not uncommon result of the ever-changing times; it induced people to relocate to other parts of the country in search for a better life, in the process killing their hometowns forever.

NOTES

1. Moses Strong to James B. Campbell, November 8, 1847, Moses M. Strong Mining Papers.

2. Schaefer, "Muscoda, 1769–1856," 35.

3. Muldoon, *Alexander Hamilton's Pioneer Son*, 143.

4. Murphy, *Gathering of Rivers*, 114.

5. Rodolf, "Pioneering in the Wisconsin Lead Region," 343.

6. Rodolf, 347.

7. Kinzie, *Wau-Bun*, 148.

8. Rodolf, "Pioneering in the Wisconsin Lead Region," 348.

9. Edgar Hamilton to Cyrus Woodman, n.d., Woodman MSS.

10. Muldoon, *Alexander Hamilton's Pioneer Son*, 142.

11. Schafer, *Wisconsin Lead Region*, 101–102.

12. Meeker, *Early History of Lead Region of Wisconsin*, 272.

13. "Wiota Town and Village."

14. Muldoon, *Alexander Hamilton's Pioneer Son*, 69.

15. Neighbour, "'Some-Time-Back' Series."

16. Conley, "Early History of Lafayette County," 326.

17. Muldoon, *Alexander Hamilton's Pioneer Son*, 144.

18. "Wiota Town and Village."

19. Buley, *Old Northwest Pioneer Period*, 343.

20. Whitford, "Early History of Education in Wisconsin," 331.

21. Muldoon, *Alexander Hamilton's Pioneer Son*, 174–175.

22. Schafer, "Muscoda, 1769–1856," 35.

23. Schafer, 39.

24. "Wiota Town and Village."

25. Schafer, *Wisconsin Lead Region*, 108.

SIX

Taming the Frontier

THE PANIC OF 1837 WAS THE WORST ECONOMIC CRISIS Americans would face until the Great Depression of the next century. Many Americans became unemployed, the cost of living went up, wages decreased, and businesses shut down forever. The financial strain hurt most Americans and lasted several years, creating a panic in the nation.

In the 1780s, the Jeffersonian Republicans had opposed a federal banking system on both philosophical and political grounds. The Federalists, on the other hand, supported a national bank. The first Bank of the United States became defunct in 1811 when its twenty-year charter expired. What followed was an ever-growing divide between the followers of Thomas Jefferson and Alexander Hamilton. But by the end of the War of 1812, the Jeffersonian Republicans began to realize the need for such an institution. With support from House Speaker Clay, Congress passed a twenty-year charter for the second Bank of the United States in 1816. The bank grew through the "Era of Good Feelings" and even survived the Panic of 1819, but by the 1830s trouble was brewing for it under the leadership of President Jackson.

Born in 1767, Jackson grew up to become a successful lawyer in Tennessee, and he later served in the US House of Representatives and Senate. He was heralded as the hero of the Battle of New Orleans during the War of 1812, and that acclaim led him to the White House in 1828. Jackson began his duties as a representative of the common man. By the 1830s, the rivalry between the Jeffersonian Republicans (now Jacksonian Democrats) and the Federalists (or the Whigs, under the leadership of Clay) grew to great proportions. The Whigs accused Jackson of using his veto power to do his own bidding without consulting Congress. With each new policy passed under the Jackson administration, the animosity between the two parties escalated.

Jackson fought a major policy battle during his second term as president: the rechartering of the second Bank of the United States. Born in 1786 to a prestigious Pennsylvania family, Nicholas Biddle graduated from Princeton University and served as secretary to President James Monroe, as US minister to Great Britain, and as president of the second Bank of the United States. Even though the bank was a private organization, Biddle ran it as a government monopoly. Jackson viewed any bank, and any debt for that matter, as an evil set by the rich against the poor. In this, he was supported by William's own brother, James Hamilton, who questioned the constitutional validity of the second Bank of the United States. When the bill for rechartering the bank appeared before Jackson in 1832, he vetoed it without any hesitation. As a populist president, he garnered support for his decision because Americans continued to believe he was the best representative of the average American.

By 1833, Jackson had removed federal government deposits from the second Bank of the United States and deposited the money in select state banks. This decision led to an increase in land speculation as Americans tried to nab more western land. With the surplus revenue from the land sales, Jackson was able to fulfill his vision of paying off the nation's debt. But the unenforced banking regulations, along with Jackson's executive order calling for all payments for land sales to be made in specie, contributed to the Panic of 1837. When Jackson's vice president, Martin Van Buren, became president of the United States in 1837, he refused to overturn Jackson's policies, which only made things worse for the economy. America remained in a deep recession until 1843.

During Jackson's presidency, transformations were also occurring in the Midwest. By 1834, Michigan was attempting to become a state. It succeeded and became independent of the Michigan Territory, in 1837. In the meantime, anticipating Michigan's statehood, the US Congress created the Territory of Wisconsin from land that once had been part of the Michigan Territory. Included in the land mass were the future states of Wisconsin, Minnesota, Iowa, and portions of North and South Dakota. The nineteen-year-old secretary and acting governor of the Michigan Territory, Stevens T. Mason, issued a proclamation on August 25, 1835, calling for an election of a legislative body for the region that would remain outside the state of Michigan. According to the proclamation, the counties of Brown and Milwaukee made up the first district and could elect five members to the Legislative Council, the county of Iowa became the second district and could elect three members, the county of Crawford became the third district and could elect one member, the county of Dubuque became the fourth district and could elect two members, and the county of Demoine became the fifth district and could elect two members. The "Rump Council" was called to meet at Green Bay on January 1, 1836.

But there was a battle over the Ohio and Michigan boundary. The Northwest Ordinance of 1787 had already established an east-to-west line from the southern tip of Lake Michigan, crossing Lake Erie and passing north of the Maumee River. Ohio recognized this line in 1803 when it drafted its constitution, adding that Ohio's northern boundary would include the mouth of the Maumee River. When the Michigan Territory was created in 1805, the US Congress incorrectly assumed the line would stay north of the mouth of the Maumee River. Congress accepted Ohio's constitution without making a final decision on the boundary question. Meanwhile, despite Ohio's claims, Michigan remained in control of the Toledo Strip. When Michigan prepared for statehood on December 11, 1833, the battle for the boundary line was rekindled. Ohio blocked Michigan's statehood until it recognized Ohio's boundary. The bloodless war between Ohio and Michigan Territory would continue for thirty years. A survey of the boundary was ordered in 1812 to end the conflict, but the War of 1812 prevented any surveying. Other surveys were ordered, one in 1817 by the surveyor general of Ohio and another by the governor of Michigan Territory, Lewis Cass. But the parties were unable to reach an agreement.

In 1833, Mason tried to offer a solution, but it was rejected by Ohio's governor, Robert Lucas. By 1835 Ohio had established Lucas County within the region under dispute. Mason ordered the Michigan militia to take over the area by force if necessary. On the Ohio side, Lucas sent the Ohio militia to fight for what they believed to be their land.

Mason sought President Jackson's help, and Jackson obliged by sending a total of two federal representatives to negotiate with the representatives of Ohio and Michigan. Unable to come to a peaceful compromise, Mason ordered his men to arrest Ohio's representatives. Jackson's representatives proposed that Ohio and Michigan govern the area together. Ohio agreed but ordered its militia to take the area by force if Michigan refused to cooperate. For his part, Mason refused to accept the proposal. Mason's handling of the boundary issue with both the federal government and the state of Ohio cost him his position as governor of Michigan Territory. In August 1835, Jackson decided to relieve Mason of his duties, replacing him with John S. Horner.

A Democrat born in Virginia, John S. Horner was a lawyer and politician. Not only did he replace Mason as secretary and acting governor of Michigan Territory, but in 1836 he became secretary of the newly formed Wisconsin Territory. Even before taking his new position, Horner decided to overthrow Mason's proclamation, releasing one of his own requiring the "Rump Council" to meet in Green Bay on December 1, 1835, instead of January 1, 1836.[1]

The election was held on October 6. Unlike most of his brothers, who were Jackson men, William was a staunch Whig and an admirer of Henry Clay. He ran as a Whig candidate from Iowa County. Despite the country's bent toward the Jacksonian Democrats, and perhaps to some extent because of his father's name and his own political experience in Illinois, William was elected to office.

When the time arrived for the council to meet, there was much confusion and frustration because of the changes in the date. The delegates felt that Horner had "allowed only twenty-one days" from the date of his proclamation for the council to meet. It was difficult enough for information to travel in good weather, let alone the harsh Midwestern winter that they had just experienced. If Horner had any understanding of the region, he would have thought about it before making his proclamation. Indeed, "any man of rational comprehension needed not to have been told of its expediency." Making matters worse, Horner was absent from the meeting on the date he himself had set up. Horner's secretary published his excuse in a local newspaper, stating that Horner "considers it a matter of more importance that they should be represented in Congress than that the Legislative Council should assemble." Many members of the council found Horner's excuse "frivolous and insufficient."[2] In the end, disregarding Horner's proclamation, William and the other legislators decided to sit out the December 1 date and meet at the January 1 date that was originally set by Mason.

During the session, William challenged the council to demand an explanation from Horner: "It is an unpleasant task for one branch of the government to examine into the conduct of its co-ordinate branches, but there are cases when it becomes an imperious duty." He felt that "the executive is not the officer of the people, but receives his appointment from another government from which, it is true, we derive our existence; for us now to be silent, when the best interests of our people are trampled upon, would be basely surrendering our rights and convincing the world that we are unworthy of the confidence of our constituents." Therefore, as their duty to the people, William felt that the council should question the manner in which Horner had behaved and issued his proclamation and that although it may "be too heavy a dose for His Excellency," it was something that must be done. He was unwilling to overlook the snub, and he thought that, far from being ignorant, Horner was a crafty fellow: "Too much in that paper is attributed to ignorance—it ought to be called 'design.' On the 9th of November Horner issued his proclamation to convene the Council for divers good reasons—but what they are he has not told us."

William continued, "[Horner] did know—that the day would arrive before the proclamation could be received; and thus he intended to defeat the session." But Horner was unavailable to give any explanation because he was "waiting at Detroit to perform an act for your benefit, which was not by law made his duty, but made expressly the duty of another! To be plain, we speak the truth when we say that he did not intend that the Council should meet, and that he has attempted to gull our constituents." Horner's inability to attend a meeting he himself had called to session showed "little respect" for the "members" who all showed up in an "inclement season of the year" and "over such extent of wilderness for no purpose."[3] The council drafted a resolution asking President Jackson to remove Horner from office, and William himself delivered the message to Washington.[4] But much to the frustration of William and the others, Jackson refused to replace Horner.

Since Horner was missing from the meeting, the council was limited in the decisions it could make. The men focused on securing printers for the council, electing members for various committees, administering the oath of office, and discussing where the seat of government for the new territory should be installed. William made the first motion to form a committee of three "to receive and decide upon the credentials of the members elect; and that the persons ascertained by the said committee to have been elected by the people be sworn as members of this Council." On January 2, William motioned for the rules of the Sixth Legislative Council to be adopted for the Rump Council or the Seventh Legislative Council. The rules were adopted. Next, the members voted to elect a president. William was "duly elected" as council president by a vote of 8 to 1. Because William left few words of his own to posterity, his brief speech during this occasion is included below to give an understanding of how he handled a position of authority:

> Gentlemen—Honored by being called to preside during the deliberations of the session of this Legislative Council, every exertion shall be used on my part to perform the duties with promptness and fidelity. The delicate relations that we bear to the general government and to the Peninsula—the numerous and varied interests of our extensive country, of its rapidly increasing population, connected to our own peculiar existence—requires the exercise of the utmost moderation and caution, at the same time firmness; the duties of the chair, growing out of these circumstances, with those

of any ordinary session, are so great that I could scarcely expect to sustain
myself and preserve the dignity of the station, but for the unanimity and
good feeling that exist throughout; relying therefore upon your kindness
and friendly disposition to aid me, it leaves a hope of being enabled to act
as will produce the end you desire. Gentlemen, you will accept my sincere
thanks for the honor conferred by your unanimous suffrages.[5]

Other officers were elected, and a committee of two was formed to
communicate with Horner. The meeting was then adjourned until later
in the afternoon, perhaps with the hope that Horner might make an
entry or provide instructions. Horner, for his part, remained in Detroit.

During the Rump Council, William also pressed for Cassville to
become the seat of government in Wisconsin. He felt that it was "the
point most convenient of approach and will best fill the various interests of the entire territory, and unite the bonds of union between
its different ports." Furthermore, he noted that such an appointment
would keep the spread of slavery in check by maintaining the "happy
balance of power . . . between the slave and non-slave-holding States."
He considered slavery an "evil" befallen on Americans and hoped
that "the government will never legislate so as to make it necessary
to violate its faith, nor, spreading slavery farther over our fair land,
root the evil deeper and deeper among us."[6] After much deliberation
and heated debate from both proponents and opponents, William's
proposal was adopted.

The council lasted fifteen days. During some of that time William
suffered from an unknown illness, but he was still present for most
of the deliberations. For his service, he earned $112.50, and an ad-
ditional $30 for the extra services he provided as president of the
council, but he was never paid. Some members accused the fiscal
agent, James Duane Doty, of cheating them. Although William had
his own reservations about Doty, on this occasion he came to Doty's
defense and admitted that "while we may differ in our opinions, and
that, too, most honestly and sincerely; but still good feelings should
be preserved." William reminded the others that "[they] came here . . .
without any prospect of receiving expenses. It was supposed perhaps
that the agent considered it a duty to the country to do what he could
to aid the Council in holding a session. He has done so, and for my

part I regard it in the light of a meritorious act." William told them that Doty had asked him how much money the council needed to defray the necessary expenses, and that William had informed him it required "a small sum for printing, stationery, etc., but the pay of members would not...be expected." Therefore, as far as William was concerned, at least in this case, Doty had "acted in good faith" and deserved the benefit of doubt.[7]

His work done at the council, William turned his attention back to taking care of his business. He owned a local newspaper called the *Free Miner's Press*, which later became a Democrat Party publication.[8] He remained involved in politics, and in 1840 he offered his support to the Whig candidate in the presidential race, William Henry Harrison. On Harrison's entry into the White House in 1841, William was hopeful for his own political career. But his hope remained unrealized because President Harrison died from pneumonia within a month of taking office.

Harrison's death elevated Vice President John Tyler into the office of president. He became the first acting vice president to replace a president. Although Tyler ran with Harrison for elected office in the famous "Tippecanoe and Tyler Too" campaign, he was anything but a puppet for the Whig Party. Unable to reach a compromise with Clay on the banking question, Tyler found himself on the outside of the party he had once represented. His maneuvering of members within the Whig Party led to a rift between southerners who supported states' rights including slavery and their opponents who were instead in favor of northern business interests. William, who had hoped to become Tyler's replacement for Dodge as the new governor, was disappointed when the president chose Doty to fill the position instead.

Born in Salem, New York, in 1799, James Duane Doty studied law and later moved to Detroit. He worked as a secretary to Michigan's governor Lewis Cass, and by 1823, he had gained the position of judge, covering the area from Mackinac to the Mississippi. During his tenure under Cass, Doty had undertaken an expedition to explore the Wisconsin region. His interest in land speculation continued to grow as the years progressed.

By 1832, Doty was relieved of his position, and he served as a member of the Legislative Council from 1833 to 1835 in the Michigan Territorial Council. Once Michigan gained statehood and the Wisconsin Territory was created, Doty had hoped to become governor of the new territory. Instead, Jackson appointed the hero of the Black Hawk War, Henry Dodge, as governor. Having lost the opportunity for public office, Doty worked on a new venture: making Madison the seat of government for Wisconsin.

As early as 1836, he had played a crucial role as a land speculator and purchased approximately a thousand acres of land that would become the city of Madison. To convince legislators to vote for Madison as the capital of Wisconsin Territory, Doty sold them choice lots in the area. This maneuvering succeeded in canceling William's suggestion of making Cassville the seat of government for the Wisconsin Territory. In the process, Doty made many friends and many more enemies. But Doty was politically savvy, and by 1841 he had beaten his rivals and acquired the governorship, an office he had wanted for a long time. His win had made William even more determined for the next election: "We have been beaten altho' in a large majority in the Territory . . . the unfortunate appointment of J. S. Doty and his conduct as executive but we must not despair next year is to fix the political cast of the Territory therefore let me urge constant action on the part of our friends." He persuaded his friends to "collect all the facts against Doty" to remove him from office.[9] But Doty served his full term as governor of Wisconsin Territory, whereas William served as a member of the House of Representatives from Iowa County from 1842 until 1843.

In 1840, William was struggling with health issues. He had just recovered from a "fever and ague."[10] By 1841, he suffered from rheumatic pains, which were worsening and required him to rest more often. John Cornelius wrote to his mother in March that same year that William "has been quite sick and has not recovered yet, he looks very thin and is in bad health."[11] In 1845 he asked Moses M. Strong to check in on a court case because he was suffering from a "severe attack of congestive fever from which I am not yet so far recovered as to induce me to think I can make my appearance at court."[12] Again, in February 1848, he told Tweedy, "My health has been very bad in fact I was so sick as to be confounded." He had been suffering from a terrible cough. By May of the same year, the cough seems to have reappeared, and William was considering "some more congenial climate in the course of the summer for my health still continues very indifferent I am now suffering with a very severe cough which ... must soon terminate my career."[13]

Despite his health issues, William resurfaced as a candidate for the 1847 Wisconsin Constitutional Convention. The day before the election, he wrote to tell his friend Tweedy that "my engagement as candidate for the convention has demanded all my time."[14] Iowa County had been reorganized earlier in the year, and William's place of residence now fell under the jurisdiction of Lafayette County. Thus, when he ran for office, he ran against John O'Conner, a Pennsylvania transplant who had just arrived in Lafayette County in 1846. To William's surprise, O'Conner won by 436 votes to William's 434. Later, William discovered discrepancies in the counting of the ballots. He challenged the nomination by petitioning the convention. Democrat member Daniel G. Fenton presented William's petition to the convention on December 16, 1847, and a select committee was chosen to investigate the issue. The convention set a date to hear both parties involved.

On January 17, 1848, William addressed the convention with a speech on his right to the seat held by O'Connor. He "claimed that illegal votes were cast for the said John O'Connor" at the ballot box. He also challenged the legality of the "poll held at Schullsburg" because "it does not appear the judges of election were sworn as the law prescribes, and the place where the votes were taken was not such a place as the law requires." O'Connor too presented his facts through his attorney. In the end, the committee found that "the election was fairly conducted, and that no fraud was attempted or committed." Therefore, they decided in favor of O'Connor. William had lost again.

For a man who had been one of the foremost pioneers handling the affairs of Wisconsin as a territory, it was a hard blow to be refused participation in the deliberations for a constitution for the state.[15] William went back home to Wiota, never to return to the political arena again. But his biggest challenge was yet to come, and when it did appear, he characteristically plunged ahead.

NOTES

1. Schafer, *Proceedings of the State Historical Society of Wisconsin*, 68:63–64.

2. Schafer, 68:93.

3. Schafer, 68:105–106.

4. Muldoon, *Alexander Hamilton's Pioneer Son*, 155.

5. Schafer, *Proceedings of the State Historical Society of Wisconsin*, 68:69–70.

6. Schafer, 68:78–79.

7. Schafer, 68:146.

8. Blair, *Annotated Catalogue of Newspaper Files*, 164.

9. William Stephen Hamilton to John Hubbard Tweedy, October 10, 1841, Tweedy MSS.

10. John Cornelius Adrian Hamilton to Maria Eliza Van den Heuvel Hamilton, September 14, 1840, private collection of Douglas Hamilton.

11. John Cornelius Adrian Hamilton to Maria Eliza Van den Heuvel Hamilton, March 1, 1841, private collection of Douglas Hamilton.

12. William Stephen Hamilton to Moses M. Strong, October 4, 1845, Woodman MSS.

13. William Stephen Hamilton to John Hubbard Tweedy, February 10, 1848, and May 30, 1848, Tweedy MSS.

14. William Stephen Hamilton to John H. Tweedy, November 28, 1847, Woodman MSS.

15. Wisconsin Constitutional Convention, *Journal of the Convention*, 319–320.

SEVEN

El Dorado

THE END OF THE MEXICAN-AMERICAN WAR IN 1848 AND the signing of the Treaty of Guadalupe Hidalgo led to the acquisition of new land for the United States, most notably California. Manifest Destiny played a vital role in the ideology of many people in the nineteenth century, but for most of the forty-niners, including William, the westward movement meant hunting for gold instead of promoting any ideological philosophy. Some traveled for other reasons, including land acquisition, business prospects, health, evasion of the law, an end to debt, and a new life away from meddling relatives or friends. Unlike believers in Manifest Destiny, these people ventured forward to explore the new territory more in hopes of finding opportunities to improve their lives than of advancing the supposedly superior Anglo-American race.

The largest American mass migration of the nineteenth century came on the heels of the discovery of gold in California at Sutter's Mill in 1848. On January 24, 1848, James Marshall discovered the first gold nugget at a sawmill construction site near the American River that he was inspecting for John Sutter. By March, news had spread in the area, but few people beyond California paid any attention to the rumors. Within a few months, however, reports reached the East Coast. In December President James K. Polk gave a speech confirming the existence of an abundance of gold in California—all of which inspired the Gold Rush of 1849. Hordes of new people arrived in the area, more than doubling the population of California in a few months.

There were a few different ways people could travel to California. The easiest way, preferred by most people, was to sail around Cape Horn. It was also one of the slower ways, taking as long as eight months to get to California. That was undesirable for most forty-niners, who were eager to get to their destination. Another route involved leaving from an Atlantic port and traveling through Panama. Although this was perhaps the fastest way to reach California, it was also more expensive. The least expensive but perhaps the most difficult was the overland journey. It required travelers to arrive at certain jumping-off points from which the actual travel to California began. Although some pioneers chose to travel using the Santa Fe Trail, most chose the California-Oregon Overland Trail. Beginning at the Missouri River, travelers crossed the Great Plains, passed the Rocky Mountains, and then headed to California or the Oregon Territory. The last stretch of the journey over the California desert was especially grueling for most travelers, and many came out of it changed forever.

To be sure, people were already living in California before the arrival of the forty-niners. Native Americans, Californios, Mexicans, fur trappers, soldiers, and thrill seekers had all paved the way to the West, but it was the forty-niners who actually set off the westward movement toward "El Dorado" at a grand scale. Men left behind families, land, and all they had ever known in hopes of finding economic freedom and stability through their adventures in the land of gold. They were the true trailblazers of the California Gold Rush.

The term *forty-niners* applies to all those who traveled to California in the wake of the California Gold Rush in 1849, including those who came from Europe, China, Australia, New Zealand, and Hawaii and crossed the Pacific Ocean to reach California. Others, such as the Mexicans from Sonora, which had once been part of Mexico, were already prospecting for gold in 1848, but more arrived in 1849. These travelers are known as forty-niners because of the year, 1849, in which they traveled to California, but they nicknamed themselves the Argonauts after the Greek myth of Jason and the Argonauts. In this myth, Jason is on a quest to find the Golden Fleece, just as the forty-niners were on a quest to find gold. Forty-niners included men from all social and economic backgrounds. Professionals such as lawyers, doctors, preachers, and politicians marched alongside merchants, miners, and vagrants.

Traveling overland to the West in the early nineteenth century required strategic planning and preparation. It could take a few days to several months from the time a person made the decision to go to California to when they actually started on the road towards their destination. Moreover, the journey itself could take several months to complete. Therefore, many people left at a time when they expected the least amount of trouble. Most tried to make the journey in the warmer months so they would have enough time to reach California before winter crept in and ruined the fodder for the animals or made the roads impassable.

The overland journey was similar for most travelers, and many people recorded their journey in journals, letters, and diaries. If William recorded his experience, the writings are lost to history. Therefore, we must rely on the firsthand accounts of his contemporaries to sketch conclusions about the overland journey he took that year.

Many settlers considered overland travel dangerous. With Fremont's map and the Mormon guidebook as possibly their only helping aid, settlers had some reason to be concerned. Fear of Native American attacks, diseases, lack of water and food, harsh weather, and terrible road conditions all required consideration. Most travelers formed groups, or companies, to travel together as part of a caravan, both for companionship and for protection. Seventeen-year-old Lucius Fairchild traveled from Wisconsin to California and wrote home to his family telling them, "We shall get all the Wisconsin teams together and form a company to travel to gether I think there will be about 50 teams from there."[1] William was captain of one of those fifty teams that may have joined others, including Fairchild's team, out of Wisconsin. Sixty men and three women traveled to California under William's command.[2]

There were various reasons that may have motivated William to go to California in 1849. After suffering defeat in his challenge to the convention in 1848, he may have decided to remove himself from the territory for some time. William spent a good majority of the winter in 1848 preparing for his journey. Included in his gear may have been a beautiful needlepoint made for him by his mother.[3] In the spring of 1849, he attached a red wagon to a team of black horses, packed them with the necessary equipment for the journey, and headed west.[4] Dr. Lord noted seeing William and his "four-horse team of fine looking animals" in his journal. William had purchased "oats to feed them, brought from Salt Lake at one dollar a bushel and threshed them himself at that."[5]

Like many other forty-niners, William may have also decided to go to California to improve his health. To be sure, he was an active and robust young man, but as he grew older, he developed physical ailments. As early as 1841, he complained about rheumatic pains and a severe cough. In the nineteenth century, fresh air was often considered therapeutic, believed to prevent many illnesses, and prescribed as a means to better health.[6] Many of the travelers hoped to find a cure or at least relief for their ailments. In a narrative published in 1908, forty-niner Edward Washington McIlhany recalled leaving Virginia for the West to look for adventure but also to overcome discontent: "One motive which caused this desire, as disappointment in my first love affair, I wanted to get far, far away, and try to forget."[7] Miner John Carr left Peoria, Illinois, accompanying others, noting that one man in his group suffered from an illness: "D.C. Young was a merchant of Chillicoathe, Illinois, who was taking the trip for his health. He was a consumptive, and his physicians told him there was no chance for his life if a trip across the plains would not help him."[8] Forty-two-year-old Alonzo Delano left his family behind in Ottawa and traveled to California for both gold and improved health: "My constitution had suffered sad inroads by disease incident to western climate, and my physician frankly told me, that a change of residence and more bodily exertion was absolutely necessary to effect a radical change in my system—in fact that my life depended upon such a change, and I finally concluded to adopt his advice."[9]

Land and business prospects also drove emigrants to move to the West. In a letter dated March 3, 1849, John H. Purdy, possibly a banker or printer from Columbus, Ohio, pointed out the benefits of owning an acre of land in California, which he felt was a "profitable employment to a mess of six persons."[10] Purdy seems to have been more interested in acquiring land than hunting for gold. Likewise, Elijah Allen Spooner, a prospector from Adrian, Michigan, said a heartfelt goodbye to his beloved wife and son and left for the West in hopes of improving their future by acquiring land in California:

> The severest parting having taken place a fortnight previous with my Family. Consisting of a Wife dearer to me than all else the world possess & or whom I would cheerfully toil the livelong day & a little innocent Boy just old enough to begin to reciprocate a Parents fondness, these are separation which tries the hardest heart, and causes the more sympathetic one to writhe in anguish which can only be known by experience But I trust of our parting will be for our mutual good, or benefit, at least, so far as property is concerned, this being the object sought Could I be assured that my life with that of my wife & little one would be spared so that we should all meet again in our little family group.[11]

There is no evidence that William wanted to move to California on a permanent basis. Lead mining in Wisconsin had reached a new phase. Already by 1847, experienced miners such as William realized that they would need more money to operate a lead mine. William wanted to go to California to find enough gold to acquire new technology to run his lead mine. He had told his friends "that he would make his way to the Pacific Coast, find his share of the gold, and return in two years."[12]

William remained a bachelor all his life, and his closest relatives lived in New York. At the age of eighty, his mother had just managed to make the journey from New York to the Midwest with his sister Eliza and her husband, Sidney Holly. More than a decade later, William's hope of ever seeing his aged mother again depended on his ability to travel to New York quickly. The people who mattered most to him—friends and neighbors whom he considered family—lived in Wisconsin. A trip to California appeared favorable to William as a way to raise funds to help his "family" and his community on his return. At his age, William wanted to remain close to the people he cared about, as is evident from his intention to return home within two years and from his last thoughts about Wiota on his deathbed.

People traveling to the West often rendered their professional services on the trail. Doctors, blacksmiths, wheelwrights, and barbers all served fellow travelers. They were often considered a welcome part of the overland experience. Lawyers helped settle legal matters as they traveled. Failing to perform guard duty on the trail, for instance, was considered a grave error, and lawyers defended fellow emigrants on such occasions. David Rohrer Leeper traveled from South Bend, Indiana, and found himself fortunate to have the services of a "witty and brilliant attorney" when he was charged with failure to respond to his call to perform guard duty.[13] Other lawyers transacted matters of legal business for their clients through the course of the journey. Here, William too may have played a part, using his expertise as a lawyer to settle matters of dispute between the travelers.

More men than women journeyed to California in 1849. Among them, the miners came in droves. Some miners were simply "overenthusiastic and feverish" with the idea of finding gold and were willing to head to California at any cost. Leeper felt that the group of people he traveled with had a romanticized notion of the West because "the hardships and perils likely to be incident to such a journey were given scarcely a passing thought."[14] As an experienced lead miner in the Midwest, William was well equipped for the "gold fields" of California, but others were ill prepared to meet the harsh realities of the overland journey, and many failed before they ever reached their destination.

Among the forty-niners, single young men often traveled by forming their own companies; others shared the journey with traveling families. Leeper traveled with such men; "the oldest was twenty-five, the youngest seventeen."[15] As a young man, William Lewis Manly of Wisconsin accepted the offer of a traveling forty-niner family for board in exchange for his hunting skills, which provided them with game on the journey: "I was, of course glad to accept this offer, and thanks to Mr. Bennett's kind care of my outfit, was better fixed then any of the other boys."[16] Josiah and Sarah Royce allowed two single young men to join them on their westward journey in exchange for extra protection: "We had traveled but a few days when, after camping one evening, we saw approaching a couple of young men, scarcely beyond boyhood, having with them a horse and a mule. They also had launched out alone, and would be very glad to keep in company with us. As they appeared civil, and one of them rather gentlemanly, we of course did not object."[17] Many such single men were widowers or unmarried brothers, beaus, and sons venturing to the West in 1849. William was fifty-two years old and had lived in Wisconsin for almost twenty years of his adult life when he decided to leave for California. As a single man he too may have benefited from the companionship of fellow travelers. The desire to reach California was of the utmost importance to all miners regardless of their age, and they made whatever accommodations they could to make the journey west.

Information on African Americans traveling overland to the West in 1849 remains limited, although there are brief accounts of them traveling with the others. In some cases, African Americans made enough of an impression on other overlanders to receive a mention in their diaries and journals. At least one African American forty-niner traveled with Leeper's train to California: "Somewhere in this section a squad of Diggers came to our train, and, seemingly for the first time, laid eyes upon a black man. Their astonishment and curiosity were unbounded. They peered up his sleeves, down his back, into his bosom, and lifted his trousers'-leg, to assure themselves that there was no hoax about the matter—that the cuticle was really black, and black all over."[18] Most other African American forty-niners were slaves traveling with their masters.

There are two versions of who accompanied William on his trip to California. One version states that aside from the team he traveled with, William went to California with his servant, an African American man named Barney Norris. Between the years 1826–1834, Norris had served John Quincy Adams as a footman. Then, in 1834, he relocated to Galena as a servant to Captain Thomas C. Legate, who was then the superintendent of the lead mines. William probably befriended Norris when he came to work in the lead mines in Galena. Norris stayed with William in California until the latter's death; thereafter, he returned to Galena and spent the remainder of his years serving as sexton at the First Presbyterian Church.[19] But Edgar Hamilton wrote favorably about another of William's African American servants named Davy. According to Edgar Hamilton's autobiography, Davy "idolized" William, and William "crossed the Rocky Mountains to California with his devoted servant"; thereafter, he "died in Sacramento . . . attended by his servant to the last."[20] So, which of the two men was with William when he left for and stayed in California? It is possible that he may have had two servants traveling with him. It is also possible that perhaps Edgar Hamilton may have confused two different people when he set out to write his autobiography many years later. What is known is that when Woodman was trying to locate William's grave, he requested Stephenson to interview Norris. Stephenson had reported the details of his interview with Norris to Woodman through his letters. Aside from Edgar Hamilton's autobiography, there is no other mention of an African American man named Davy who may have known William or traveled to California with him. One thing is certain, whether it was Norris or Davy, there was at least one faithful African American friend by William's side when he died.

The fear of Native American attacks was of prime concern for most travelers moving to the West. Many people during this period held a jaundiced view of Native Americans because of the fear spread by gossip, literature, and newspaper articles about the supposed massacres on the overland trails. They also believed that all Native American people were homogenous, which only added to their fear of all Native Americans in general.

Contact between the travelers and Native Americans was inevitable in 1849, although contagious diseases had wreaked havoc on many of the tribes.[21] Their interactions are notable in that they were unlike Hollywood portrayals. To be sure, fights did occur, but they were sporadic and often resulted from misunderstandings between the emigrants and Native Americans instead of from any premeditated attack.[22] The truth about the actual relationships between the Native Americans and the forty-niners lay somewhere in the middle of aggression and admiration.

Forty-niner men in particular held mixed feelings about Native Americans. Some found them to be a nuisance; others considered them an amazing group of people. Lorenzo Dow Stephens of Illinois thought that the Native Americans were incorrigible beggars, saying, "Indians seem to be hungry at all times."[23] Leeper was even more vicious in his attacks on the Native Americans:

> Along the Humboldt River, we were annoyed more or less with the visits of squads of the Digger Indians; a type chiefly distinguished for their filthy habits, repulsive appearance, and pilfering propensities. Their inflictions upon the emigrants up to this time had been chiefly in the way of persistent begging and petty stealing; but, later in the season, their depredations took a more serious turn, in the way of running off and slaughtering stock, and sometimes in attacking and killing the emigrants themselves. When left to their own resources, they seemed to subsist mainly on the fat black crickets of the valley and the plenitude of their own vermin.[24]

But Edmund Booth, a farmer from Iowa, held a different opinion of the Native Americans he befriended on his overland journey in 1849. Booth met a handful of "Truckee's Indians," who he found as the most "civilized" and "agreeable fellows."[25] He also noted that when his team was passing through Nebraska, "our train was stopped by Indians" who "demanded ten dollars for the privilege of going across their country" as another group of about "two hundred others, men, women, and children stood or moved about" nearby. At this point, William, who served as the captain of Booth's team, commanded the men and women in the team to "get ready their arms" and then he "gave the order to start" moving forward. At this point, the Native Americans moved aside and let them pass through and "there was no further trouble from the Indians."[26] Herman Scharmann, a businessman from New York who was equally enamored with the Native Americans, said, "I was very much drawn to this man, because of his unusual physiognomy and behavior," and "I experienced real regret at having to leave these savages who appeared to me to be more civilized than many so called civilized men."[27] Friendships did occur between some Native

Americans and travelers on occasion, even if they did not last long. In moments of hostility, people found ways to cooperate and deal with one another. Friction occurred because of fear, anxiety, and unfamiliarity with other cultures, but at least during this period, the travelers and Native Americans were more likely to help than to harm one another. William's experiences and understanding of Native Americans and their culture in the Midwest may have helped him in any dealings he had with individuals from other tribes during his journey.

Most people traveling overland used a prairie schooner, or covered wagon, pulled by oxen. Made with wooden frames, the wagons were covered with heavy cloth to provide protection. Although they did not provide passengers with the most comfortable ride, they did provide enough space to carry equipment and to allow a family to sleep or rest if necessary. Many people walked alongside their wagons all the way to California. William took at least one red wagon, perhaps more, to California with him.

In addition to the oxen pulling the wagons, people also took horses, pigs, milk cows, mules, and even dogs on their journey. Of course, domesticated animals were not the only ones around. The travelers often hunted rabbits, squirrels, prairie dogs, bison, deer, antelope, rattlesnakes, and other wild animals for food as they journeyed west.

The weather was of great significance to the people traveling to California. The terrain on the overland trail was typically rough, with uneven roads and treacherous rivers. Many travelers complained of a continuous onslaught of rain through the course of their journey. Forty-niner Delano was astounded by the terrific thunder and lightning he experienced on the trail: "Peal after peal rolled along, as if heaven's artillery were doing battle, and soon flood-gates were opened upon us in a perfect deluge."[28] Leeper complained about being "beset with mud, slush and flood incident to the breaking up of winter" from the beginning of his journey.[29] Even when travelers managed to avoid the storms, their animals often suffered instead. One afternoon, Lell Hawley Woolley, a pioneer from Vermont, noticed that his animals had taken a thrashing from the fierce storms on the trail: "There came up one of those terrible hailstorms, common in that country, which pelted the mules with such severity as to cause them to take fright and run away, breaking loose from the wagons which were taken by the storm in another direction, first wheels up, then top, until the latter was all in rags; then they stopped. When we came into camp at night they looked sorry enough and you would have thought they had just come out of a fierce fight."[30]

The rain not only made the road difficult to travel but also left an unbearable chill in the air. Manly and his companions had to huddle together as "pigs" to stay warm, and even then the emigrants were often left wet and cold.[31] On the morning of May 7, 1849, E. S. Ingalls from Lake County, Illinois, woke up chilled to the bone after a frigid night: "Had a bad night last night; it rained and snowed nearly all night. Had about two inches of snow on the ground this morning."[32]

Most of the people dressed the same way as they had back at home. Woolen shirts, flannel underclothes, and jeans kept their bodies warm. Topped with hats and heavy boots, they tried to keep dry by using wool blankets when confronted with the harsh weather.

Perhaps the most dreaded part of the trail was the monstrous Forty Mile Desert. The extreme high and low temperatures made the climate harsher, dangerous even for the bravest of them. This massive expanse of dry land was unavoidable. The best-planned journey could easily turn into a disaster once a train reached the Forty Mile Desert. Carr wrote that the heat in the desert was "oppressive," and the drifting sand was so thick that the wheels of his wagon were buried almost ten inches deep within it.[33] Manly added that the desert produced "no living creature," and he was certain that the travelers on his train were about to die from starvation in the sea of desert unfolding before their eyes.[34]

Trekking across the Forty Mile Desert was hazardous for most people. Water was often the most needed resource, and also the most difficult thing to find. The Humboldt River flowed nearby, but the water was unsafe to drink because it had an overabundance of poisonous minerals. Many people suffered because they either miscalculated the extent of the trek through the desert or simply ran out of water during their crossing. Of all the adverse conditions the travelers experienced, thirst was the most commonly noted complaint. Stephens stated that unquenchable thirst was "the most agonizing suffering possible and the feeling is indescribable."[35] Others such as Manly felt that both people and animals suffered gravely because of the absence of water on the westward trail.[36]

Some travelers did prepare well for their journey. Flour, bacon, biscuits, cornmeal, coffee, tea, and sugar were all packed tight on their wagons. Wood provided the fuel necessary to cook food, but as Fairchild wrote, when wood was unavailable food was cooked "with Buffalo chips."[37] Buffalo chips or cow chips were manure droppings from the particular animal used as a secondary source of fuel on the overland trail. Knives, rifles, rope, soap, nails, needles, and thread were also considered essential for the journey. Those who did not know any better packed formal wear, books, and furniture. As the journey grew long and weary, they tossed away many of the items. Pioneers often found discarded items along the way.

For those who were ill prepared, the lack of food often brought just as many problems as did the scarcity of water. Those who had rushed on their journey with only meager provisions hoped that they might borrow from other travelers.[38] When faced with hunger, many people resorted to eating whatever they could find just to survive. Stephens noted that emigrants on his train ate wild animals because they were on the verge of starving: "We were out five or six days following up the creek to its source, in fact went clear to the summit of the mountain, but we ran out of grub and for three days had nothing to eat but chipmonks, at least what little there was left after shooting them with a rifle."[39] Things were so horrible for Manly and other travelers on his train that they resorted to eating raw hide: "Two or three yards of it at a time, was cut into pieces about five inches long, the hair singed off, the sand scratched out, and these pieces were dropped into our camp kettle and cooked until the whole formed one mass of jelly or gluten which was, to us, quite palatable."[40] Delano was amazed to learn about a man traveling to California on foot who essentially survived on prairie dogs and the kindness of fellow emigrants.[41]

When people ran out of food and begging produced undesirable results, many resorted to violence.[42] Scharmann recorded that he aimed
his pistol at a man who refused to sell him provisions and threatened
to "shoot him like a dog."[43] Even when they were able to acquire food,
many travelers suffered from food-related illnesses, making it virtually impossible to obtain the nutrients needed to stay alive. Stephens
was so malnourished that he was mere skin and bones: "Upon remov-
ing my clothes I was actually frightened. I found I was nothing but a
skeleton.[44] Even if they somehow survived, lack of food and malnutrition over time often led to disastrous results.

Illness was a major problem for people on the overland journey.
Diseases such as diarrhea, tuberculosis, smallpox, and mumps were
often present on the overland trail, but cholera, mountain fever, and
scurvy were the most serious.[45] Scharmann stated that the most common illness on the trail were "dysentery, intermittent fever, cholera,
and scurvy."[46] Cholera in particular was widespread on the overland
trails in 1849, by far the worst year of westward migration to experience an enormous breakout of the deadly disease. In this sense, the
forty-niners were again unique compared to emigrants of later years.
Cholera spread through unclean food and water. Those suffering from
it experienced severe vomiting, diarrhea, high fever, chills, dehydration, and muscle cramps. Stephens noted: "The cholera was bad that
year. I am satisfied that there were many people who died with fever
as with cholera, for, once attacked death seemed certain."[47] Kimball
Webster, a young farmer and miner from New England, witnessed the
killer disease in action when he stopped over in Independence, Missouri, in May: "The Asiatic cholera was raging among the immigrants
to a large extent. Many were daily falling victims of this dreaded
scourge; many others were becoming disheartened and were turning
back to their homes."[48]

Scurvy was the next most bothersome disease the forty-niners acquired during their overland journey, followed close by mountain
fever. Inadequate diet and lack of proper hygiene contributed to these
diseases. According to Manly, scurvy was a "common complaint"
at this time, usually prevented or cured by eating raw potatoes and

onions.[49] Many people believed this to be a quick remedy and followed the treatment plan. Mountain fever was dangerous too, although, with proper care, a person had a chance to survive. Men in Carr's train became sick from mountain fever, which added to their problems: "We worried along all that day, nothing but sand all around us, and, to make matters worse, two of our men were taken down with the mountain fever and had to be hauled in the wagon."[50] It was possible to survive these diseases, but many people were left feeling weak even if they made it through the illness.

In the face of so many hardships, it was common for tempers to flare at the slightest provocation. Travelers on Leeper's train wandered off until only a few of the original remained, and even they were aloof and disinterested in caring for others: "Parching winds and stifling dust, with the bountifully blotched and blistered lips that afflicted nearly every one in consequence, did not at all conduce to that geniality of temper that would incline men to social solace."[51] A man on Delano's train brutally murdered another over a petty misunderstanding: "A reckless villain named Brown, requested a young man who acted as cook in his mess, to get him a piece of soap. The young man was at the moment bending over the fire, engaged in preparing the meal, as he was busy. With out further provocation, as it appeared the wretch raised his knife and stabbed him in the back, killing the young man almost instantly."[52] Considering some of the hardships travelers faced, their perplexing behavior becomes somewhat understandable. The loss of loved ones, property, hope, and health was detrimental in many ways to those traveling to the West in 1849.

Physical hardships on the overland trail were disheartening. Morale was often low. To keep things cheerful, sometimes the pioneers used music and dancing by the campfire as a way to distract themselves. Leeper wrote that his group was "able to muster several instruments— violin, banjo, tambourine and castanets" to ward off melancholy.[53] But despite such efforts, the breakdown of the mind, which was even worse than physical discomfort, often followed. Stephens found men on his train who had lost hope and become mentally ill: "He seemed a little off in his mind, and by the way, there were two in our party who never did get entirely in their right minds again."[54] Many people became so overcome with grief over a lost loved one that they were incapable of handling reality. John Woodhouse Audubon, a painter and second son of the famous ornithologist and painter John James Audubon, traveled from New York to the West. During his journey, he handled the burial of a fellow forty-niner because the dead man's brother was in shock: "I had to prepare him for burial, for his brother was too prostrated with grief to do anything."[55] At such moments, the kindness of fellow travelers helped those who became inconsolable. The loss of a loved one was probably the most difficult part of the journey for them.

Many people recovered from the shock, but others could not maintain their commitment to the treacherous journey and wanted to return home. The loss of morale can shake most people facing adversity, and the forty-niners were no exception. Stephens regretted having left home to go to California, having "never felt so much like backing out of any undertaking."[56] In her book *Travels in the United States, Etc.*, English poet and writer Lady Emmeline Stuart Wortley wrote, "What misery has this California emigration brought on thousands of families—unknown, incalculable wretchedness!"[57] Indeed, the few forty-niner women who traveled during this period were often dejected, and even if they somehow made the journey, most of them hated the memory of their travel. Manly wrote that women especially "contracted a strange dislike" of the area and "never wanted to see any part of it again."[58]

Back in Wisconsin, the loss of many of its most experienced miners, including William, had adverse consequences. Land prices declined with rapidity as people sold their plots in a hurry. Lead prices increased because of the shortage of miners. Families who were left behind had to adjust to the absence of the men of the house. In addition to their roles as homemakers, women also had to take over the running of farms and businesses. Children often stepped in to help by providing the necessary manual labor. Some families held on to the hope of resuming their lives as before, but others gave up on the return of their husbands, sons, brothers, and fathers. Yet despite the changes in society, farming and mining continued to grow as new immigrants arrived to replace the miners who had left.

The discovery of gold in California beckoned people to leave everything they knew behind in hopes of finding gold and a better future. William traveled to California for much the same reason as any other forty-niner. Although many failed in their quest to reach California, those who survived found that the true test of their journey lay ahead, in the land of El Dorado.

NOTES

1. Fairchild, *California Letters of Lucius Fairchild*, 16.
2. Booth, *Edmund Booth (1810–1905) Forty-Niner*, 14.
3. "Obituary of Col. Wm. S. Hamilton," *Sacramento Transcript*.
4. Gara, "William S. Hamilton on the Western Frontier," 25.
5. Lord, *A Doctor's Gold Rush Journey to California*, 91.
6. "The Public Health Response."
7. McIlhany, *Recollections of a '49er*, 2.
8. Carr, *Pioneer Days in California*, 34.
9. Delano, *Life on the Plains and among the Diggings*, 13–14.
10. Purdy, *Trails of Hope*, 1.
11. Spooner, *Trails of Hope*, 1.
12. Muldoon, *Alexander Hamilton's Pioneer Son*, 197.
13. Leeper, *Argonauts of Forty-Nine*, 9.
14. Leeper, 2.
15. Leeper, 1.
16. Manly, *Death Valley in '49*, 106.
17. Sarah Royce, "Frontier Lady," 97–98.
18. Leeper, *Argonauts of Forty-Nine*, 31.
19. Berry, "Hamiltons," April 17, 1880.
20. Edgar Hamilton, "Autobiography of Rev. Edgar A. Hamilton," 2.
21. Unruh, *Plains Across*, 395.
22. Tate, *Indians and Emigrants*, x.
23. Stephens, *Life Sketches of a Jayhawker of '49*, 6.
24. Leeper, *Argonauts of Forty-Nine*, 24.
25. Booth, *Edmund Booth (1810–1905) Forty-Niner*, 29.
26. Booth, 14.
27. Scharmann, *Scharmann's Overland Journey to California*, 9.
28. Delano, *Life on the Plains and among the Diggings*, 26.
29. Leeper, *Argonauts of Forty-Nine*, 2.
30. Woolley, *California 1849–1913*, 3.
31. Manly, *Death Valley in '49*, 234.

32. Ingalls, *Journal of a Trip to California.*
33. Carr, *Pioneer Days in California,* 56.
34. Manly, *Death Valley in '49,* 150.
35. Stephens, *Life Sketches of a Jayhawker of '49,* 22.
36. Manly, *Death Valley in '49,* 340.
37. Fairchild, *California Letters of Lucius Fairchild,* 29.
38. Unruh, *Plains Across,* 145.
39. Stephens, *Life Sketches of a Jayhawker of '49,* 13.
40. Manly, *Death Valley in '49,* 297.
41. Delano, *Life on the Plains and among the Diggings,* 108.
42. Unruh, *Plains Across,* 147.
43. Scharmann, *Scharmann's Overland Journey to California,* 17.
44. Stephens, *Life Sketches of a Jayhawker of '49,* 28.
45. Unruh, *Plains Across,* 408–409.
46. Scharmann, *Scharmann's Overland Journey to California,* 14.
47. Stephens, *Life Sketches of a Jayhawker of '49,* 6.
48. Webster, *Gold Seekers of '49,* 35.
49. Manly, *Death Valley in '49,* 399.
50. Carr, *Pioneer Days in California,* 56.
51. Leeper, *Argonauts of Forty-Nine,* 8–9.
52. Delano, *Life on the Plains and among the Diggings,* 125.
53. Leeper, *Argonauts of Forty-Nine,* 4.
54. Stephens, *Life Sketches of a Jayhawker of '49,* 27.
55. Audubon, *Audubon's Western Journal,* 59.
56. Stephens, *Life Sketches of a Jayhawker of '49,* 2.
57. Wortley, *Travels in the United States,* 109.
58. Manly, *Death Valley in '49,* 231.

EIGHT

Dead End

ONCE THEY ARRIVED AT EL DORADO, PEOPLE WERE confronted with the harsh reality of life in California. They faced many challenges, including stiff competition, absence of decent living quarters, immorality, lawlessness, inflation, and lack of food. The gold was scarce, but the gold diggers were plentiful. There were people from all over the world—and more arriving each day. Even if travelers made it through the overland trek as William did and found a way to settle in the area long enough to prospect for gold, dangerous diseases—including diarrhea, tuberculosis, smallpox, mumps, scurvy, dysentery, mountain fever, and cholera—continued to wipe them out.

William survived all the hardships associated with overland travel and made it to California in 1849. There he settled to work in the southern region of Weaver Creek, approximately one hundred miles from Sacramento.[1] By 1849, work that had begun prior to the discovery of gold at Sutter's Mill was left incomplete. Much of the seaport looked abandoned. Shanties appeared overnight. Whereas in 1848 much of the area had been wilderness, by 1849, Sacramento had become a town built on top of a swamp. Soon, two-story buildings with barrooms on the bottom floor started popping up, with the upper rooms being let out to boarders every night. Franklin Buck, living in Sacramento at the time, described the situation to his sister: "You have no idea how this country is going ahead. Last spring there was nobody here and now the people are as thick as in the city of New York."[2] Indeed, Delano observed the same growth when he visited Sacramento, which "astonished" him because "along the road hotels and dwellings had been erected at convenient distances; and where we had traveled the previous fall without seeing a human habitation, was now the abode of civilized man."[3]

San Francisco, too, had become a boomtown. When people arrived, they often took up whatever accommodations they could find. Years later, California politician Elisha Oscar Crosby described meeting up with an acquaintance from New York who provided him with shelter in San Francisco: "He received me in a friendly way certainly, and extended the hospitality of his office, which was all he could do. He had built with his own hands a little bunk in one corner of his office where he slept himself, and told me I was welcome to lay my blankets in another corner on the floor."[4]

The growth of boomtowns such as San Francisco and Sacramento increased the population of California to over one hundred thousand by the year's end, and it was a diverse population at that. Franklin Buck noted, "You meet in the streets people of all nations. Most of them are Chilenos, Peruvians, and Mexicans."[5] Others, such as Colonel James Ayers, observed that Native Americans "of the Yaqui tribe, those stalwart aborigines who occupy the fairest part of Sonora" were also mining.[6]

The population increase led to fierce competition. Colonel Richard Barnes Mason, who was appointed to the military command in 1848 in California, sent reports back to Washington stating, "The new discovery of these vast deposits of gold has entirely changed the character of Upper California. Its people, before engaged in cultivating their small patches of ground, and guarding their herds of cattle and horses, have all gone to the mines."[7] The competition in turn brought along a surge of inflation in the cost of supplies.

The basic equipment necessary to mine for gold included the stamp iron pan, pick, and shovel. The pick and shovel were used to break up rocks and remove dirt. The stamp iron pan was a flat-bottomed pan used to scoop pebbles and dirt from water and to filter out the gold from the debris. Some miners used a cradle to transport the debris from the streams and then rocked the cradle to filter out the gold. Even for a seasoned miner such as William, it was a filthy, grueling, and frustrating job. Men had to work with efficiency and care during the sifting process because haste led to the loss of small pebbles of gold. During the hot summer, men worked without paying attention to heat exhaustion and dehydration. In winter, things were also bad, as dropping temperatures caused exhaustion and hypothermia. Yet men continued to labor because they believed hard work and perseverance would bring success. Indeed, this proved to be the case for William. By the end of the year, he had saved up a tidy sum of $12,000.[8]

As an enterprising man, William did not limit himself to digging for gold; he also opened a common goods store in Weaver Creek to supply other miners with tools and supplies.[9] A typical common goods store sold food, clothes, boots, and mining supplies. Most goods sold at high prices, as Crosby noted: "Sheet iron, tin cups, pans and tin ware of various kinds, nails, and articles of that kind . . . proved to be just the things wanted in the mines," and they "sold at most fabulous prices."[10] Considering his intention of returning to Wisconsin, to save money, William too may have charged top prices for the items he sold.

Immorality and lawlessness ran rampant through many of the boomtowns. Possibly because of his experience and the general respect men seem to have had for him, William offered to create some sense of balance in the mining community. On Saturday, January 5, 1850, Dr. Lord recorded in his journal that "a man came to notify us of a meeting to be held, on account of an assault committed on a man of the name of Nichols, in his own 'diggings.'" He discovered that "a number of persons had convened, elected a magistrate and constable and adjourned to Col. Hamilton's house." When Dr. Lord went there, he "found the house jammed full." They were in the process of hearing the Nichols case, and "when the jury were out, a meeting was organized, and a committee was appointed to draft resolutions to be reported on Saturday evening next, on the subject of claims." In the meantime, Nichols's case "was conducted with the best kind of feeling, the only aim being to establish the truth, and do justice to all."[11]

In a male-driven society, without the responsibilities of a family, many of the miners found it easier to spend the money they made from the gold on unwise pursuits. A heavy presence of saloons, gambling establishments, and brothels kept quite a few miners busy, but not all of them lost their minds with gold fever. More than thirty years after William's death, Cyrus Woodman chided William's nephew Schuyler Hamilton for calling his uncle a gambler and found his opinion "a gross aspersion upon his uncle's character, and [it] should not have been made." Woodman, who had known William for a decade in the Midwest, insisted that William "was not a gambler during any part of the time when I knew him and I believe that he was never a gambler." But he admitted that although William was a "temperate man," he was not "a 'temperance man.'"[12] Perhaps William frequented such establishments as others had done, but, again, he was more interested in prospecting for gold and returning back home.[13]

Some miners may have shared William's desire to return home, but others continued to spend their money on the gaming table at the local saloon instead of prospecting for gold. Delano recalled, "A change had been gradually coming over many of our people, and for three or four days several industrious men had commenced drinking, and after the monte bank was set up, it seemed as if the long smothered fire burst forth into a flame. Labor, with a few exceptions, seemed suspended, and a great many miners spent their time in riot and debauchery."[14] To be sure, prostitution flourished in boomtowns; even as some miners tried to remain faithful to their wives or fiancées, many more succumbed to their sexual desires. Alcoholism, loneliness, peer pressure, and even boredom all contributed to the downfall of many of the forty-niners.

As California experienced a population growth with the incoming emigrants, it also witnessed a rapid increase in its number of deaths because of disease and malnutrition. Men dropped dead faster than others could find a burial spot for them. Many were buried in a haphazard manner, and their bodies were never found again.

In 1850, William's luck ran out, and he too succumbed to the cholera outbreak that had already killed many people. Five years later, Woodman, trying to gather information about William, contacted a friend named Samuel Rich in Sacramento, California. He asked Rich to find out "whether any gravestones mark the spot where Col. Wm. S. Hamilton was buried" and, if William's grave was unmarked, to "confer a great favor on [Woodman] by having the grave marked so that it can be found when gravestones are ready." Woodman added that if there "are no stones and the grave can be found," he would "immediately upon hearing from [Rich], have gravestones prepared."[15] Rich responded two months later, telling Woodman, "After some examination I found the grave of Co. W. S. Hamilton" in a potter's field, and "his name is cut with A Knife on A small piece of board: and registered No 50 there is nothing on the board but his name and No 50." Years later, Samuel's son George Rich followed up with Woodman in a letter written on September 27, 1878, describing William's last hour: "He was laying on a cot in a back room little furniture if any there. It appeared a solitary and lonely place for a sick man . . . The Col. The impression I have was taken down with the dysentery: in a bad form."[16] In a letter written in 1880 to Woodman, George Gratiot noted that he had spoken to the physician who attended William in his illness and that Dr. Crouin had told him that "Col. Wm. S. Hamilton was attacked with malarial fever."[17]

Speculations about the day and cause of William's death have existed since the nineteenth century. Today, records suggest that he died on one of the following dates: August 7, 1850; October 7, 1850; or October 9, 1850. He is said to have died from dysentery, cholera, malarial fever, heart disease, or even murder. Since keeping good records was of the least importance in 1850s California, it has been difficult to assess the accuracy of any given date or cause of death. After his research, Muldoon was convinced that William died from cholera on August 6–7, 1850.[18] Through the course of research for this book, I reached a different conclusion.

On June 25, 1900, an old acquaintance, James Howe, claimed to have seen William for the last time on July 30, 1850, in California. In a letter to the *Sacramento Union*, Howe described in detail his last meeting with William. Furthermore, he shared his suspicions that William might have been murdered by some of his neighbors for his gold.[19] The *Daily Alta California* listed August 7, 1850, as William's date of death.[20]

However, William's old friend Barney Norris, who was with William when he died, stated in 1877 that William had died on October 7, 1850.[21] Furthermore, Dr. Lord recorded in his journal on Monday October 7, 1850 that William "died today at a quarter to 12 M. of heart disease—Co. Wm. S. Hamilton, youngest son of Alexander Hamilton."[22] An obituary in the *Sacramento Transcript* of October 8, 1850, reported Monday, October 7, 1850, as the date of William's death. The same paper reported William's death as Monday, October 7, 1850, in the October 15, 1850, issue.[23] Indeed, this was the same obituary that was copied over in the *Daily Alta California* mentioned before, with one exception: the date of death was changed to "Monday the 7th August" from the *Sacramento Transcript*'s date of Monday, October 7, 1850.

Furthermore, although Rich had stated that William died on August 7, 1850, years later he insisted that October 9, 1850, was William's correct date of death and that his illness "was not long, may of lasted two weeks."[24] George Gratiot was uncertain about an exact date of death but told Woodman that William died "about 6 weeks after you left."[25] Almost thirty-eight years later, in a letter to a mutual friend named Longfellow, Woodman mentioned that he had visited William in Sacramento "about ten days before he died" and that when he saw William, the man had been "sick."[26]

The first recorded outbreak of a cholera epidemic in Sacramento began on October 8, 1850, when a man came off a ship that had docked; however, it is possible that cholera was already making its rounds in Sacramento. If William died on August 7, 1850, how did his death go unreported for two months? Granted, during the 1850s things often fell through the cracks, but to announce a person's death in a local newspaper obituary two months later seems odd even by nineteenth-century standards. Moreover, on the basis of the testimony of

Norris and Dr. Lord's journal entry, two men who were both present when William died, and the report published in the *Sacramento Transcript* of October 8, 1850, it seems logical that William contracted cholera sometime in late September or early October 1850. Had he died on October 9, 1850, the *Sacramento Transcript* could not have published his obituary a day in advance. Furthermore, on October 8, 1850, Dr. Lord jotted in his journal that the day was "cloudy and quite cool this morning. Some thunder and a smart shower at half past 2 p.m. Immediately after followed the remains of Col. H. to their last resting place, and before we left the grave there was another shower." This indicates that Dr. Lord was not only present when William died but also at the graveside when William was buried—both events that he recorded in his journal.[27] Also, the *Sacramento Transcript* states that William died on a Monday. A check of the calendar for the year 1850 shows that only October 7, 1850, was a Monday. Both August 7, 1850, and October 9, 1850, were Wednesdays. Given all these facts, the most probable date of William's death is October 7, 1850.

William's death is tragic not only because he suffered but also because he died alone in a place that was not his home. It was two years before his youngest brother Philip could visit William's grave in California. His mother never knew of her son's death.[28] No last words were spoken over his grave at the time of his death by any of his family members.

It was Woodman, William's friend and political rival, who took it upon himself to honor William's memory by procuring information about his final days. In 1856, William's sister Eliza thanked Woodman for his "beautiful interference in a friend's behalf."[29] At Woodman's request, Stephenson found Norris and interviewed him about William's whereabouts and his final hours. Stephenson then reported his findings to Woodman in a letter: "He always regretted having come to California. . . . He was washed and shaved, nicely draped in a black suit. . . . His remains were hauled to the grave in a furniture wagon. . . . I did not see or knew of any clergyman being present. . . . He was buried in the then public grave yard."[30]

More than twenty years after his death, William finally had a tombstone set on his grave. Woodman had ordered a "Granite Slab" from
O. M. Wentworth: Monument Works of Boston on March 29, 1871,
to be placed on the grave of his deceased friend and had paid $106.80
to cover the costs.[31] Stephenson noted that if not for all Woodman
had done on William's behalf, "a few years of neglect additional no
one living could tell where he was buried."[32] Those who attended
the placement service included, among others, William's old friend
George T. Rich.[33]

William's restlessness in life followed him well after his death.
Since his original burial, William has been "exhumed twice" and
buried "three times in three different locations." Today, his grave is
located in a designated spot called Hamilton Square on the grounds
of the Old City Cemetery in Sacramento, California. It is surrounded
by a lush garden full of sweet-smelling roses and perennials.[34] William's last wish to return home to Wisconsin and to his friends and
family was never fulfilled. Instead, he lies in a place he considered
loathsome.

Although William left many questions about himself unanswered,
the study of his life provides us with the opportunity to understand
the lives of many others who lived during that ever-evolving period.
To be sure, William was the son of a great American, but in many
ways, he was a great American himself. Although he never acquired
the same level of political fame as his father, William embraced his
father's ideals of hard work and perseverance. He believed in pos-
sessing a spirit of entrepreneurship, kindness, and valuing merit over
pedigree. He led men in war, and without hesitation rolled up his
sleeves to work beside them in the mining fields as a common laborer.
He created solutions for challenges such as settling towns, employing
workers who needed jobs, helping family and friends in need, and
constructing weapons to ward off enemies. Above all, William lived
his life on his own terms. In many ways, William is the quintessential
American, and in discovering him, we may just be able to find a bit
of ourselves.

NOTES

1. Muldoon, *Alexander Hamilton's Pioneer Son*, 202.
2. Buck, "Trading for Dust," 43.
3. Delano, "Living Dead in Califor-nee," 115–116.
4. Crosby, "The Rush Begins," 56.
5. Buck, "Trading for Dust," 42.
6. Ayers, "Rich Diggings," 90.
7. Mason, "Official Report to the US Government," 30.
8. Muldoon, *Alexander Hamilton's Pioneer Son*, 202.
9. Muldoon, 202.
10. Crosby, "The Rush Begins," 60.
11. Lord, *A Doctor's Gold Rush Journey to California*, 208.
12. Cyrus Woodman to W. Longfellow, September 26, 1888, Woodman MSS.
13. Muldoon, *Alexander Hamilton's Pioneer Son*, 208.
14. Delano, "Living Dead in Califor-nee," 122.
15. Cyrus Woodman to Samuel Rich, October 8, 1855, Woodman MSS.
16. George Rich to Cyrus Woodman, August 27, 1878, Woodman MSS.
17. George Gratiot to Cyrus Woodman, April 8, 1880, Woodman MSS.
18. Muldoon, *Alexander Hamilton's Pioneer Son*, 208.
19. Muldoon, 205–208.
20. "Obituary of Col. Wm. S. Hamilton," *Daily Alta California*.
21. Charles L. Stephenson to Cyrus Woodman, December 26, 1877, Woodman MSS.
22. Lord, *A Doctor's Gold Rush Journey to California*, 301–302.
23. "Obituary of Col. Wm. S. Hamilton," *Sacramento Transcript*.
24. Muldoon, *Alexander Hamilton's Pioneer Son*, 209; George Rich to Cyrus Woodman, August 27, 1878, Woodman MSS.
25. George Gratiot to Cyrus Woodman, April 8, 1880, Woodman MSS.
26. Cyrus Woodman to W. Longfellow, September 26, 1888, Woodman MSS.
27. Lord, *A Doctor's Gold Rush Journey to California*, 302.
28. Edgar Hamilton to Cyrus Woodman, January 23, 1880, Woodman MSS.
29. Elizabeth Hamilton Holly to Cyrus Woodman, February 13, 1856, Woodman MSS.
30. Charles Stephenson to Cyrus Woodman, December 26, 1877, Woodman MSS.
31. O. M. Wentworth Jr. to Cyrus Woodman, receipt, March 29, 1879, Woodman MSS.
32. Charles Stephenson to Cyrus Woodman, January 8, 1880, Woodman MSS.
33. "Local Intelligence."
34. "Hamilton Square Perennials."

Bibliography

MANUSCRIPT AND ARCHIVAL SOURCES

Hamilton, Edgar A. "Autobiography of Rev. Edgar A. Hamilton." Unpublished manuscript, private collection of Douglas Hamilton.

Hamilton, John Cornelius Adrian. "Letters." Unpublished manuscript, private collection of Douglas Hamilton.

Illinois State Archives, Springfield, Illinois.
  Hamilton, William Stephen. "Contracts with Surveyors." Illinois State Archives, RG 953.004, May 17, 1820.

Library, Archives, and Museum Collections, Wisconsin Historical Society, Madison, Wisconsin
  Cyrus Woodman Papers.
  John Hubbard Tweedy Papers.
  Smith, M. *William S. Hamilton.* Wisconsin Historical Society, 3458, 1880.

Lincoln Collection, Abraham Lincoln Presidential Library and Museum, Springfield, Illinois.
  Hamilton, William Stephen. "Promissory Note to Edward Dick Taylor." SC 638, 1825.

Peoria Historical Society Collection, Bradley University—Cullom-Davis Library, Peoria, Illinois.
  Dixon, John. "First Plat of Peoria." Peoria Historical Society Collection, Bradley University Library, 1826.

Rare Book and Manuscript Library, Columbia University, New York, NY.
  Hamilton Family Papers.

Polhill, Norman Lee. "William S. Hamilton, Pioneer in the Old Northwest." Master's thesis, Western Illinois University, 1964.

BOOKS

Adams, John. *My Dearest Friend: Letters of Abigail and John Adams.* Edited by Margaret A. Hogan and C. James Taylor. Cambridge, MA: Harvard University Press, 2007.

Anderson, Robert. "Reminiscences of the Black Hawk War." In *Wisconsin Historical Society,* vol. 10, 167–176. Madison, WI: Democrat Printing, State Printer, 1888. http://content.wisconsinhistory.org/cdm/compoundobject /collection/whc/id/4988/show/4589/rec/1.

Audubon, John W. *Audubon's Western Journal: 1849–1850: Being the Ms. Record of a Trip from New York to Texas, and an Overland Journey through Mexico and Arizona to the Gold Fields of California.* Cleveland: Arthur H. Clark, 1906. http://archive.org/stream/audubonswesternj00audufo.

Ayers, James. "Rich Diggings." In *Gold: Firsthand Accounts from the Rush That Made the West,* edited by John Richard Stephens, 83–90. Guilford, CT: TwoDot, 2014.

Baringer, William E. *Lincoln Day by Day: A Chronology 1809–1865.* Vol. 1. Washington, DC: United States Lincoln Sesquicentennial Commission, 1960. https://archive.org/stream/lincolndaybyday01unit.

Black Hawk. *Life of Black Hawk.* New York: Dover, 1916.

Blair, Emma Helen. *Annotated Catalogue of Newspaper Files in the Library of the State Historical Society of Wisconsin.* Edited by R. G. Thwaites and I. S. Bradley. Madison, WI: Democrat Printing, State Printer, 1898.

Booth, Edmund. *Edmund Booth (1810–1905) Forty-Niner: The Life Story of a Deaf Pioneer, Including Portions of His Autobiographical Notes and Gold Rush Diary, and Selections from Family Letters and Reminiscences.* Stockton, CA: San Joaquin Pioneer and Historical Society, 1953. https://www.loc.gov/item/53003517/.

Brookhiser, Richard. *Alexander Hamilton, American.* New York: Free Press, 1999.

Brunson, Alfred. "Memoir of Thomas Pendleton Burnett." In *Wisconsin Historical Society,* vol. 2, 233–325. Madison: Wisconsin Historical Society, 1856. http:// content.wisconsinhistory.org/cdm/compoundobject/collection/whc/id/4415 /show/4144/rec/41.

Buck, Franklin. "Trading for Dust." In *Gold: Firsthand Accounts from the Rush That Made the West,* edited by John Richard Stephens, 35–54. Guilford, CT: TwoDot, 2014.

Buley, R. Carlyle. *The Old Northwest Pioneer Period, 1815–1840.* Vol. 1. Bloomington: Indiana University Press, 1978.

Carr, John. *Pioneer Days in California: Historical and Personal Sketches.* Eureka, CA: Times Publishing, 1891. http://www.archive.org/stream /pioneerdaysincaloocarr.

Chapman, Chas. C. *The History of Fulton County Illinois.* Peoria, IL: Chas. C. Chapman, 1879. https://books.google.com/books?id=udfVAAAAMAAJ.

Chernow, Ron. *Alexander Hamilton.* New York: Penguin Books, 2004.

Crosby, Elisha Oscar. "The Rush Begins." In *Gold: Firsthand Accounts from the Rush That Made the West,* edited by John Richard Stephens, 55–66. Guilford, CT: TwoDot, 2014.

Delano, Alonzo. *Life on the Plains and among the Diggings: Being Scenes and Adventures of an Overland Journey to California; With Particular Incidents of the Route, Mistakes and Sufferings of the Emigrants, the Indian Tribes, the Present and the Future of the Great West.* Auburn, NY: Miller, Orton and Mulligan, 1859. http://www.archive.org/stream/lifeonplainsamoodela.

———. "Living Dead in Califor-nee." In *Gold: Firsthand Accounts from the Rush That Made the West,* edited by John Richard Stephens, 111–126. Guilford, CT: TwoDot, 2014.

Draper, Lyman C. "The Story of the Black Hawk War." In *Wisconsin Historical Society,* vol. 12, 216–275. Madison, WI: Democrat Printing, State Printer, 1892. http://content.wisconsinhistory.org/cdm/compoundobject/collection/whc/id/7286/show/7007/rec/9.

Fairchild, Lucius. *California Letters of Lucius Fairchild.* Madison: State Historical Society of Wisconsin, 1931. https://tile.loc.gov/storage-services//service/gdc/calbk/004.pdf.

Ford, Thomas. *History of Illinois.* Chicago: S. C. Griggs, 1854. https://books.google.com/books?id=GAyA6ninhBQC.

Gratiot, Adele. "Mrs. Gratiot's Narrative." In *Wisconsin Historical Collections,* vol. 10, 261–275. Madison, WI: Democrat Printing, State Printer, 1888. http://content.wisconsinhistory.org/cdm/compoundobject/collection/whc/id/4988/show/4694/rec/75.

Greene, Evarts Boutell, and Clarence Walworth Alvord. *The Governor's Letter Books.* Vol. 4 of *Collections of the Illinois State Historical Library.* Springfield: Trustees of the Illinois Historical Library, 1909. https://books.google.com/books?id=oWUOAAAAIAAJ.

Grignon, Augustin. "Seventy-Two Years' Recollections of Wisconsin." In *Wisconsin Historical Society,* vol. 3, 195–295. Madison, WI: Calkins and Webb, 1857. http://content.wisconsinhistory.org/cdm/compoundobject/collection/whc/id/1793/show/1528/rec/222.

Hamilton, Alexander. *Alexander Hamilton: Writings.* Edited by Joanne B. Freeman. New York: Library of America, 2001.

Hamilton, Allan McLane. *The Intimate Life of Alexander Hamilton: Based Chiefly upon Family Letters and Other Documents.* New York: Charles Scribner's Sons, 1911.

Hamilton, James A. *Reminisces of James A. Hamilton: Men and Events at Home and Abroad during Three Quarters of a Century.* New York: Charles Scribner, 1869. https://archive.org/stream/cu31924032756136.

Harrison, S. A., and Oswald Tilghman. *Memoir of Lieut. Col. Tench Tilghman, Secretary and Aid to Washington: Together with an Appendix, Containing Revolutionary Journals and Letters, Hitherto Unpublished.* Library of Congress. Accessed July 25, 2019. https://www.loc.gov/resource/lhbcb.22944/?sp=1.

History of Sangamon County, Illinois: Together with Sketches of Its Cities, Villages, Townships; Portraits of Prominent Persons, and Biographies of Representative Citizens. Chicago: Interstate, 1881. https://books.google.com/books?id=jY8UAAAAYAAJ.

Houck, Louis. *A History of Missouri from the Earliest Explorations and Settlements until the Admission of the State into the Union.* Chicago: R. R. Donnelley and Sons, 1908. https://archive.org/stream/historyofmissour03houc.

Ingalls, E. S. *Journal of a Trip to California by the Overland Route across the Plains in 1850–51.* Waukegan, IL: Tobey, 1852. http://www.archive.org/stream /journalofatript031780gut/31780-8.txt.

Ingersoll, R. G. *History of Peoria County, IL: Containing a History of the Northwest—History of Illinois—History of the County, Its Early Settlement, Growth, Development, Resources, Etc., Etc.* Chicago: Johnson, 1880. http://books .google.com/books?id=j4w6AQAAIAAJ.

Jung, Patrick J. *The Black Hawk War of 1832.* Norman: University of Oklahoma Press, 2007.

Kinzie, Juliette August Magill. *Wau-Bun.* New York: H. W. Derby, 1854. https:// quod.lib.umich.edu/m/moa/aja2903.0001.001.

Leeper, David Rohrer. *The Argonauts of Forty-Nine, Some Recollections of the Plains and the Diggins.* South Bend, IN: J. B. Stoll, 1894. http://cdn.loc.gov//service /gdc/calbk/032.pdf.

Levasseur, Auguste. *Lafayette in America in 1824 and 1825.* Translated by Alan R. Hoffman. Cambridge, NH: Lafayette, 2006.

Lord, Israel Shipman Pelton. *A Doctor's Gold Rush Journey to California.* Edited by Necia Dixon Liles. Lincoln: University of Nebraska Press, 1999.

Manly, William Lewis. *Death Valley in '49: Important Chapter of California Pioneer History; The Autobiography of a Pioneer, Detailing His Life from a Humble Home in the Green Mountains to the Gold Mines of California; and Particularly Reciting the Sufferings of the Band of Men, Women and Children Who Gave "Death Valley" Its Name.* San Jose: Pacific Tree and Vine, 1894. http://www.archive.org/stream /deathvalleyin49100manl.

Mason, Colonel Richard. "Official Report to the US Government." In *Gold: Firsthand Accounts from the Rush That Made the West,* edited by John Richard Stephens, 21–34. Guilford, CT: TwoDot, 2014.

McIlhany, Edward Washington. *Recollections of a '49er: A Quaint and Thrilling Narrative of a Trip across the Plains, and Life in the California Gold Fields during the Stirring Days following the Discovery of Gold in the Far West.* Kansas City, MO: Hailman, 1908. https://cdn.loc.gov//service/gdc/calbk/014.pdf.

Meeker, Moses. *Early History of Lead Region of Wisconsin.* Madison: State Historical Society of Wisconsin, 1872. http://content.wisconsinhistory.org/cdm /ref/collection/tp/id/50850.

Muldoon, Sylvan P. *Alexander Hamilton's Pioneer Son: The Life and Times of William Stephen Hamilton, 1797–1850; Early New York, Missouri, Illinois, Michigan, Wisconsin, Iowa and California.* Harrisburg, PA: Aurand, 1930.

Murphy, Lucy Eldersveld. *A Gathering of Rivers: Indians, Metis, and Mining in the Western Great Lakes, 1737–1832.* Lincoln: University of Nebraska Press, 2000.

Palmer, John McAuley. *Historical and Reminiscent.* Vol. 1 of *The Bench and Bar of Illinois.* Chicago: Lewis, 1899. https://books.google.com/books?id=Zn4 _AAAAYAAJ.

Parkinson, Daniel M. *Pioneer Life in Wisconsin*. Vol. 2 of *Wisconsin Historical Collections*, edited by Lyman C. Draper. Madison: Wisconsin Historical Society, 1859. http://content.wisconsinhistory.org/cdm/compoundobject/collection/whc/id/4988/show/4694/rec/75.

Parkinson, Peter, Jr. "Notes on the Black Hawk War." In *Wisconsin Historical Society*, vol. 10, 184–212. Madison, WI: Democrat Printing, State Printer, 1888. http://content.wisconsinhistory.org/cdm/compoundobject/collection/whc/id/4988/show/4614/rec/19.

Powell, William. "William Powell's Recollections." In *Proceedings of the State Historical Society of Wisconsin at Its Sixtieth Annual Meeting*, 146–175. Madison: Wisconsin State Historical Society, 1912. https://archive.org/stream/1912procee dingsoowiscuoft#page/166/mode/2up/search/william+s.+hamilton.

Power, J. C. *History of Springfield, Illinois: Its Attractions as a Home and Advantages for Business, Manufacturing, Etc.* Springfield: Illinois State Journal, 1871. https://archive.org/stream/historyofspringoopowe.

Purdy, John. *Trails of Hope: Overland Diaries and Letters, 1846–1869*. Excerpted, BYU Harold B. Lee Library Digital Collections, 2002. Accessed March 30, 2012. http://contentdm.lib.byu.edu/cdm/singleitem/collection/Diaries/id/4257/rec/20.

Rennick, Percival Graham. "Peoria and Galena Trail." In *Journal of the Illinois State Historical Society*, vol. 27, 351–431. Springfield: Illinois State Historical Society, 1908. https://archive.org/stream/journalofillinoi27illi.

Reynolds, Cuyler. *Genealogical and Family History of Southern New York and the Hudson River Valley: A Record of the Achievements of Her People in the Making of a Commonwealth and the Building of a Nation*. Vol. 3. Cambridge, MA: Lewis Historical Publishing Company, 1914. https://books.google.com/books?id=iNIUAAAAYAAJ&source=gbs_navlinks_s.

Rodolf, Theodore. "Pioneering in the Wisconsin Lead Region." In *Wisconsin Historical Society*, vol. 15, 338–389. Madison, WI: Democrat Printing, State Printer, 1900. http://cdm15932.contentdm.oclc.org/cdm/ref/collection/whc/id/7656.

Romer, John Lockwood. *Historical Sketches of the Romer, Van Tassel and Allied Families, and Tales from the Neutral Ground*. New York: W. C. Gay, 1917. https://books.google.com/books?id=_FBPAAAAMAAJ.

Royce, Sarah. "A Frontier Lady." In *Gold Rush: A Literary Exploration*, edited by Michael Kowalewski, 97. Berkeley, CA: Heyday Books, 1997.

Salisbury, Albert. "Green County Pioneers." In *Wisconsin Historical Society*, vol. 6, 401–415. Madison, WI: Atwood and Culver, State Printer, Journal Block, 1872. http://content.wisconsinhistory.org/cdm/compoundobject/collection/whc/id/3876/show/3769/rec/74.

Salter, William. *The Life of Henry Dodge: From 1782 to 1833*. Burlington, IA: 1890. https://archive.org/details/GR_3659.

Schafer, Joseph. *Proceedings of the State Historical Society of Wisconsin*. Vol. 68. Madison: State Historical Society of Wisconsin, 1921. https://books.google.com/books?id=M_wWAQAAMAAJ.

———. *The Wisconsin Lead Region*. Madison: State Historical Society of Wisconsin, 1932. https://archive.org/stream/wisconsinleadregooscha.

Scharmann, H. B. *Scharmann's Overland Journey to California: From the Pages of a Pioneer's Diary*. Translated by Margaret Hoff Zimmermann and Erich W. Zimmermann. N.p.: n.p., 1918. http://cdn.loc.gov//service/gdc/calbk/013.pdf.

Smith, William R. "Personal Narrative of William S. Hamilton." In *The History of Wisconsin in Three Parts, Historical, Documentary, and Descriptive*, 339–342. Madison, WI: Beriah Brown, Printer, 1854. http://books.google.com/books?id=6vNJROIT-18C&pg=PA339&dq=%22William+S.+Hamilton%22&ie=ISO-8859-1#v=onepage&q=%22William%20S.%20Hamilton%22&f=false.

Spooner, Elijah Allen. *Trails of Hope: Overland Diaries and Letters, 1846–1869*. Excerpted, BYU Harold B. Lee Library Digital Collections, 2002. http://contentdm.lib.byu.edu/cdm/compoundobject/collection/Diaries/id/3591/show/2313/rec/5.

Stephens, Lorenzo Dow. *Life Sketches of a Jayhawker of '49*. San Jose: Nolta Brothers, 1916. http://cdn.loc.gov//service/gdc/calbk/148.pdf.

Street, Joseph. "The Sioux and the Black Hawk War." In *Wisconsin Historical Society*, vol. 5, 310–314. Madison, WI: Atwood and Rublee, State Printer, Journal Office, 1868. http://content.wisconsinhistory.org/cdm/compoundobject/collection/whc/id/1220/rec/6.

Strong, Moses M. "The Indian Wars of Wisconsin." In *Wisconsin Historical Society*, vol. 8, 241–286. Madison, WI: David Atwood, State Printer, 1879. http://content.wisconsinhistory.org/cdm/compoundobject/collection/whc/id/2839/rec/9.

Tanner, Herbert B. "Papers of Indian Agent Boyd, 1832." In *Wisconsin Historical Society*, vol. 12, 266–298. Madison, WI: Democrat Printing, State Printer, 1892. http://content.wisconsinhistory.org/cdm/compoundobject/collection/whc/id/7286/show/7053/rec/43.

Tate, Michael. *Indians and Emigrants: Encounters on the Overland Trails, 1840–1870*. Norman: University of Oklahoma Press, 1999.

Tillson, Christina Holmes. *A Woman's Story of Pioneer Illinois*. Chicago: R. R. Donnelly and Sons, 1919.

Unruh, John D., Jr. *The Plains Across: The Overland Emigrants and the Trans-Mississippi West, 1840–60*. Champaign: University of Illinois Press, 1993.

Washburne, E. B. *Sketch of Edward Coles, Second Governor of Illinois, and of the Slavery Struggle of 1823–4*. Chicago: Jansen, McClurg, 1882. https://archive.org/stream/sketchofedwardcooowashrich.

Webster, Kimball. *The Gold Seekers of '49: A Personal Narrative of the Overland Trail and Adventures in California and Oregon from 1849 to 1854*. Manchester, NH: Standard Book, 1917. http://www.archive.org/stream/goldseekersof49p00webs.

White, C. Albert. *A History of the Rectangular Survey System*. Washington, DC: United States Department of the Interior Bureau of Land Management, 1991. https://www.blm.gov/sites/blm.gov/files/histrect.pdf.

Whitford, W. C. "Early History of Education in Wisconsin." In *Wisconsin Historical Society*, vol. 5, 321–351. Madison, WI: Atwood and Rublee, State Printers, Journal Office, 1868. http://content.wisconsinhistory.org/cdm/compoundobject/collection/whc/id/1220/show/1084/rec/38.

Whitney, Ellen M., ed. *The Black Hawk War: 1831–1832*. Springfield: Illinois State Historical Society, 1970. https://archive.org/stream/blackhawkwar183135whit.

Wisconsin Constitutional Convention. *Journal of the Convention to Form a Constitution for the State of Wisconsin: With a Sketch of the Debates, Begun and Held at Madison, on the Fifteenth Day of December, Eighteen Hundred and Forty-Seven.* Madison, WI: W. T., Tenney, Smith and Holt, 1848. https://catalog.hathi trust.org/Record/011636035.

Wood, Gordon. *The Idea of America: Reflections on the Birth of the United States.* New York: Penguin, 2011.

Woolley, Lell Hawley. *California 1849–1913; or, The Rambling Sketches and Experiences of Sixty-Four Years' Residence in that State.* Oakland, CA: De Witt and Snelling, 1913. http://cdn.loc.gov//service/gdc/calbk/064.pdf.

Wortley, Emmeline Stuart. *Travels in the United States, Etc.: During 1849 and 1850.* New York: Harper and Brothers, 1851. https://books.google.com/books?id =Y7kTAAAAYAAJ.

JOURNALS, PERIODICALS, AND WEBSITES

"Alexander Hamilton's Son Surveyed Peoria, Platted Its Streets." *Peoria (IL) Journal-Transcript,* April 2, 1933. https://www.wisconsinhistory.org/Records /Newspaper/BA1928.

Berry, J. A. "The Hamiltons." *Peoria Freeman,* April 17, 1880.

Chroust, Anton-Hermann. "The Legal Profession in Early Missouri." *Missouri Law Review* 29, no. 2 (1964): 129–137. https://scholarship.law.missouri.edu/cgi /viewcontent.cgi?article=1849&context=mlr.

Conley, P. H. "The Early History of Lafayette County." *Wisconsin Magazine of History,* March 1919. http://content.wisconsinhistory.org/cdm/compoundobject /collection/wmh/id/28466/show/28392/rec/22.

DeForest. "Primitive Gunnery." *Sacramento Daily Record-Union,* May 29, 1884. http://chroniclingamerica.loc.gov/lccn/sn82014381/1889-05-29/ed-1/seq-4/.

"Early Lawyers of St. Louis: The First Forty Years Enrollment at the Bar." *St. Louis (MO) Republic,* June 10, 1894.

Gara, Larry. "William S. Hamilton on the Wisconsin Frontier: A Document." *Wisconsin Magazine of History* 41, no. 1 (1957): 25–28. http://content.wisconsinhistory.org/cdm /compoundobject/collection/wmh/id/26062/show/26008/rec/5.

Hamilton, William S. "Letter to John Coons." *Galenian* (Galena, IL), July 4, 1832.

"Hamilton Square Perennials." Old City Cemetery. Accessed 2015. https://www .historicoldcitycemetery.org/.

"Local Intelligence." *Sacramento Daily Record-Union,* December 13, 1879. https:// cdnc.ucr.edu/cgi-bin/cdnc?a=d&d=SDU18791213&e=------185-en--20--121--txt -txIN-william+s.+hamilton-------1.

Moon, Bill. "The Story of Nom-A-Que: Court Records Tell Interesting Story of Peoria County's First Murder Trial." *Journal of the Illinois State Historical Society (1908–1984)* 5, no. 2 (1912): 246–255. http://www.jstor.org/stable/40194013 ?seq=3.

Morrow, Lynn. "A Surveyor's Challenges: P.K. Robbins in Missouri." Southeast Missouri State University Press. Last accessed 2019. http://www.semopress .com/a-surveyors-challenges-p-k-robbins-in-missouri/.

Neighbour, L. B. "The 'Some-Time-Back' Series." Wisconsin Historical Society. Last accessed 2018. http://www.wisconsinhistory.org/wlhba/articleView.asp?pg=1&id=1930&hdl=&np=&adv=yes&ln=Hamilton&fn=William&q=Col%2E&y1=&y2=&ci=&co=&mhd=&shd=.

"Obituary of Col. Wm. S. Hamilton." *Daily Alta California*, October 18, 1850. https://cdnc.ucr.edu/cgi-bin/cdnc?a=d&d=DAC18501018.2.3&dliv=none&e=------185-en--20--121--txt-txIN-william+s.+hamilton-------1.

"Obituary of Col. Wm. S. Hamilton." *Sacramento Transcript*, October 15, 1850. https://cdnc.ucr.edu/cgi-bin/cdnc?a=d&d=ST18501015.2.13&srpos=136&dliv=none&e=------185-en--20--121--txt-txIN-william+s.+hamilton-------1.

Schafer, Joseph. "Muscoda, 1769–1856." *Wisconsin Magazine of History*, September 1920. http://content.wisconsinhistory.org/cdm/compoundobject/collection/wmh/id/2213/show/2111/rec/1.

"Seat of War." *Galenian* (Galena, IL), June 6, 1832.

"The Public Health Response." Stanford.edu. Accessed April 17, 2018. http://virus.stanford.edu/uda/fluresponse.html.

"State Capital: Proclamation." *Sacramento Transcript*, October 9, 1850. https://cdnc.ucr.edu/cgi-bin/cdnc?a=d&d=ST18501009.2.3.1&dliv=none&e=------185-en--20--121--txt-txIN-william+s.+hamilton-------1.

"Wiota Town and Village." Wisconsin Historical Society. Last accessed 2018. http://www.wisconsinhistory.org/wlhba/articleView.asp?pg=1&orderby=&id=15996&pn=1&adv=yes&hdl=&np=&ln=&fn=&q=&y1=&y2=&ci=&co=Lafayette&mhd=&shd=.

Index

A. K. FIELDING is an independent historian and an artist. She writes about early American topics so she can buy materials with which to paint subjects from that period. The author of numerous historical articles, she is also author of the A Little Book of Revolutionary Quotes series. She lives in the land of the free and the home of the brave. Visit https://trehanstreasures.com/ for more information and news from A. K. Fielding.